GW00725414

MARKETING SERVICES

A Practical Guide

John Courtis

BIM

KOGAN
PAGE

First published in 1987 as 'John Courtis on the Marketing of Services' by
Professional Publishing Limited
7 Swallow Place, London W1R 8AB

First published in 1988 by
Kogan Page Ltd
120 Pentonville Road, London N1 9JN
in association with British Institute of Management
Management House, Cottingham Road,
Corby, Northants NN17 1TT

Reprinted 1988, 1989 (twice), 1990

British Library Cataloguing in Publication Data

Courtis, John
    Marketing services: a practical guide.
    1. Organisations. Services. Marketing
    I. Title   II. British Institute of
    Management
    338.4'068'8

    ISBN 1-85091-657-8

Printed and bound in Great Britain by
Biddles Ltd, Guildford and King's Lynn

The author

John Courtis, FCA was commissioned in the RAF after qualifying as a chartered accountant in 1959; he then worked for the Ford Motor Company and later switched to Reed Executive where he was an employee/director. He set up John Courtis & Partners in 1973.

Contents

Introduction

Marketing makes selling easier, or virtually unnecessary ...

We live in a post-industrial society. There are more entries in the average *Yellow Pages* for services than for manufacturers of products. This book attempts to fill a gap in marketing literature, which has hitherto concentrated largely on product marketing.

The author has spent nearly quarter of a century in service-based businesses and draws practical examples from most of them – and from his clients' experiences.

All owners and employees of service organisations will find something here which will enhance their own and their company's performance.

This is not a conventional, structured textbook but a cheerful, even cynical, review of the marketing art and the many gaps in its practice. It is not just a book about the practice of marketing for people who work in service businesses. It is a handy pack of convertible benefits.

The aim is that readers, having read the book, will be better equipped to understand what marketing is and how better marketing can help their businesses survive, prosper and grow.

Ralph Waldo Emerson said: 'If a man write a better book, preach a better sermon or make a better mousetrap than his neighbour, though he build his house in the woods, the world will make a beaten path to his door.' The quotation, like all half-truths, is dangerous. People have got to know about your better mousetrap before they can react. Worse, if your 'product' is a service, there is often no visible evidence of its merits or even of its existence and nature.

This may be clearer if we have a common view on what marketing is. For our purpose, marketing covers every aspect of a company's affairs which makes selling possible, easier or even unnecessary.

Even Mr Emerson's quotation needed marketing. It would not now be in your *Dictionary of Quotations* but for a Mrs Sarah Yule who jotted it down for posterity when in the audience at one of his lectures. She is a classic example of an 'influencer' whose personal conviction about the product often forms a significant part of the marketing chain.

Marketing, in its turn, is arguably the most important part of the management chain, in that the business cannot exist without sales and, almost without exception, sales do not happen without some marketing taking place. Marketing takes place in the context of the business as a whole. In a service business the context is different from that of a production environment. Equally the challenge is different. You cannot easily market services as an impulse buy off the page or off the counter. You therefore need to issue your messages in a form which is memorable, or can be retained in some other form, precisely because there is no tangible product.

In a service business the product is service, and intangible. This creates a narrow structure in that most of the management functions present in a manufacturing company are largely absent. In a service business you will *not* normally find the following functions:

- procurement;
- production;
- warehousing;
- engineering;
- security;
- distribution;
- quality control; or
- research and development.

However, you *will* find:

- sales;
- marketing;

2

- finance;
- operations (i.e. the service); and perhaps
- personnel.

Each of these functions has a bearing on the way the service is recognised by customers. The effect is distilled by the fact that their contacts are all part of the service.

Marketing is fun

This book is not for marketing experts, unless they are having trouble selling marketing within their organisations (not an unusual problem, by the way).

It is intended for:

- people who do not quite know what marketing is and are put off by conventional textbooks;
- amateurs who are practising marketing already and want to do it better;
- people for whom marketing is a part of their (non-marketing) job, whether or not they realise it;
- anyone else employed in a service business who cares about profit, survival and growth.

Jerry della Femina once said: 'Advertising is the most fun you can have with your clothes on.' With respect to the doyen of the US advertising world he was, and remains, wrong. In business, marketing is the most fun. Unfortunately, many advertising people miss out because they believe that advertising is the be-all and end-all of marketing, somewhat like the sales people who believe that marketing is just a part of the sales function.

Marketing is the most fun because it embraces all the elements which enable a business to sell its product effectively. Marketing makes selling easier, or virtually unnecessary. This fact is not always appreciated because most marketing is done by people outside the marketing department, who belittle the function because they know, if unclearly, that they are doing some or all of the things the official marketing staff ought to be doing.

The only cure for this inter-departmental misunderstanding is the realisation that everyone in a business has some marketing

3

responsibility. This is true to some extent in businesses with a tangible product, but especially true in a service business where every employee's contact with the outside world may be perceived as part of the service.

Here we must clear up a semantic point. To the marketing professional what the business sells is a 'product', whether it is a tangible object or an abstract service. We shall try to ignore this convention because there are going to be numerous cases where we have to draw a distinction between services and physical products. This brings us to the first problem. Most people accept that you need to sell products. Alas, in many up-market service businesses it is considered unethical or unprofessional to sell, either because there are sector rules or traditions about cold canvassing, or because the words are not clearly understood.

Some people in these businesses think 'sell' and 'sale' are four letter words, in the pejorative sense. We shall come to them later. In the meantime even they must appreciate that marketing is not a four letter word in either sense (we say '*even* they' because people who think selling is unethical are usually intelligent and numerate members of their professions).

Marketing is, therefore, considered less unethical than selling. So far, so good. For the record, the author himself is against selling. His ideal is a situation in which buyers queue up in an orderly line, you sell them whatever product you feel like selling that day, and they all go away happy.

Even in this situation the marketing effort which has made it possible does not relieve you of the responsibility of closing the sale, and you, or they, may want to exercise some degree of choice about how they use your services, or how they pay for them, or how both sides communicate while the service is being performed. This, too, is part of marketing.

1   Negative marketing

The results of your marketing effort can be successful — or not...

Negative marketing, a somewhat forbidding phrase, describes a major conceptual breakthrough in the process of transforming an existing marketing activity or creating an effective new one. Recognising and avoiding negative marketing is the key.

Achieving this is easy to explain, less easy to implement. The results of your marketing effort can be successful – or not. Most people treat the 'or not' category as one group. This is incorrect. Even marketing professionals fail, or fear, to recognise that the 'or not' encompasses:

(a) neutral results; and
(b) damaging or wholly counter-productive ones.

Once this basic problem is recognised, it is relatively easy to introduce disciplines, checks and attitudes which reduce or eliminate the risk of practising negative marketing.

Negative marketing is often practised by people outside the marketing department who do not regard any aspect of marketing as part of their job. It is also practised by people in marketing who have forgotten their objectives.

A few examples may help. Let us start with an existing customer – your best target market unless you are selling funerals (and perhaps even then if the customer has enough geriatric relatives). We all know that successful service to the customer usually brings repeat business or recommendations. Less successful service, or a failure to make the customer aware that the service was worthwhile, brings neutral results.

Rotten service, or a tolerable service perceived as rotten, actually deters customers from coming back and turns them into ill-will ambassadors who will go out of their way to warn people against you.

Advertising can have the same effect. A distinguished clearing bank spent vast sums of money on a television campaign designed to show how sympathetic it was. During this campaign one of its branch managers had a minor customer prosecuted for exceeding her very modest overdraft limit. As the case got national publicity, the image which came into many minds each time the advertisement was screened was not of the friendly local manager lending an ear but of the unfortunate customer finding an unsympathetic police officer waiting to arrest her in the bank manager's office. That is negative marketing on a grand scale.

Equally, it is no use putting slogans like 'Let the train take the strain' and 'We're getting there' in front of commuters waiting for a train which has been cancelled. British Rail has partially recognised this, and the advertising likely to be most offensive to a freezing season-ticket holder is generally not now displayed at stations.

Direct mail

Direct mail is another major problem area. Bad direct mail from a service company is doubly harmful because there is no tangible product with a positive image to counteract the effects of the mailshot. For instance, if you receive a substandard text from a motor dealer it probably does not produce a wholly adverse impression of the car they are trying to sell you. It may reinforce your existing reservations about motor dealers, but the product reputation survives.

However, if the most tangible thing about your future service is the bad mailshot, one of the following things can happen:

- if sent to existing, satisfied customers, as if they were not yet customers, it conveys the secondary message that your research has been done badly and/or that you do not remember them as individuals;
- if sent to a less than satisfied customer, it reinforces their adverse recollection of you for the same reasons;

- if boring, it may dissuade the recipient from reading the next one, which would otherwise have been effective;
- if the mailshot is actually part of your credit control procedures, it is doubly threatening (all communications in writing to customers are part of your direct mail effort, whether finance staff recognise it or not);
- if badly integrated with the rest of the programme, it may erode or contradict what the good material is achieving.

Inherently offensive marketing is another area in which you can spend thousands of pounds on your competitors' behalf. Most readers will remember the classic Martini advertisements, in which the late Leonard Rossiter almost invariably spilt the product over Joan Collins. This campaign sold a lot of vermouth but I suggest that it may also have alienated people who are embarrassed by this type of advertising. The other problem – that it may have sold a lot of Cinzano, Campari and Noilly Prat to people who loved the advertisement but could not quite remember the name of the product – is covered in Chapter 8, Communications.

Most people are offended when their name is spelt wrongly on a direct mailshot. This is particularly true if you are selling a premium service, offering to help them with their direct mail, or using one of those tricky letters which include their name several times in the body of the text.

Negative marketing is sometimes more powerful than positive marketing. In an extreme case, not only do the potential customers decide not to use you this time, but the urge never to use you again is fixed in their subconscious. This sort of message is seldom achieved by arm's length marketing alone. It is usually achieved by providing a conspicuously bad service so that the people who should be singing your praises become your detractors. The impressions linger on. I still wince at the recollection of an incompetent estate agency, a dishonest service station, an unsympathetic dry cleaners (and shredders), several plumbers and the corporate finance head of a major clearing bank.

What can you do about negative marketing? You cannot be everywhere at once. The solution is threefold. Firstly, you should monitor your allegedly positive marketing efforts to ensure that their effects are likely to be as planned, without side-effects.

Secondly, you should educate *all* staff about the image you are trying to present and the way their face-to-face contacts and correspondence make or break that image.

Thirdly, a more general point, do not leave a vacuum. Wherever you fail to present a positive message, take positive action or give clear direction, your staff are likely to do nothing or to do something wrong. In these circumstances the ones with initiative are the most dangerous. They can be guaranteed to do something, often wrong, whereas the apathetic do nothing.

Typically, in employee communications, gossip, rumour, speculation and invention flow in to fill every vacuum left by lack of information from management. So it is with the total marketing effort. If employees do not have a clear view of their role and the company's objectives, they will operate in the wrong context.

Even marginal misunderstandings can be devastating. In one of my companies we set great store by delivering on time. This message ran through all our marketing literature. Alas, one team member had a unique interpretation of this. By his time management things got done *almost* on time. Unfortunately other people, including customers, call this late. He thought his performance was competent and reliable, but it was the sort of reliability David Niven attributed to Errol Flynn: 'You can rely on Errol. He will *always* let you down.'

This sort of problem must be solved by education or by better recruitment, or it erodes all the good marketing that is going on elsewhere.

Failure is the norm

Sir Thomas Lipton is alleged to have said that half his advertising was wasted but he could not do anything about it because he did not know which half. The same is true of marketing.

In pursuit of improvement in this area I want to recommend something I have not yet achieved in my own business, because the identification of the problem is an essential precedent to the solution, and many marketing experts do not yet accept the nature of the problem.

In brief, both experts and amateurs have got used to mediocre results from their marketing efforts. In the direct mail field, for example, it is accepted that a very small response is the norm and that moving your response rate a fraction of one per cent deserves an accolade. This is a policy of mediocrity.

Let us start from the other end. If the product is worthwhile, needed by the whole target population and unique, something close to 100% response ought to be the norm. If there is competition but your product is patently the best, something over 50% ought to be the aim. Why, then, are we satisfied with conversion rates in single figures?

There are several answers, some of them acceptable, some intolerable, and some of them certainly curable. The first is that history dictates the norm. It is easy to be satisfied with a tiny response if past experience in the trade is that one per cent is not bad and three per cent is miraculous, with the implication that 97–99% of your marketing spending is wasted. Even taking into account the defence that some of the wasted effort actually softens up the consumer for next time, the objective of a first time result remains valid.

Forget history. Failure rates of around 90% should not be the norm: they suggest that one or more of the following must be true of the marketing effort in question.

- The target market has not been correctly identified.
- The service offering has no Unique Selling Proposition (USP).
- The message was not convincing.
- The medium was wrong.
- The message was sent to the wrong place (home or office?).
- The timing was wrong (time of year, day, week).
- The way to buy or reply was not clear enough.
- The transmission of the message was in some other way defective so that the target did not receive or register it (this is not necessarily the same as the wrong medium).

Each of these defects is due to bad communication. Even the need for more research implies a communication failure.

The fact that we cannot identify an organisation which has solved all these problems fully does not mean there are no solutions. Many exist and are discussed elsewhere in the book. At this point we just need to remember the existence of such problems in order to put future efforts in context.

2   Objectives

Businesses can be remarkably hostile or cool to potential customers . . .

Marketing is not just an academic exercise. It is linked with your corporate objectives, which we assume to include profit, survival and growth. Each of these depends on a reliable income. Corporate income depends on sales. Sales depend on marketing.

Good marketing must produce enough sales at the right margins to ensure survival. Better marketing should produce better sales, to facilitate profits and growth. Better sales, in this context, must meet one or more of the following criteria. They are:

● realised in cash earlier or more easily;
● at better gross margins;
● of higher unit value;
● achieved with less marketing effort and expense per sale;
● from customers who will come back for more and/or recommend the company to others.

Achieving better sales may permit the business to be more profitable on the same turnover, with less working capital. Other things being equal, it is usually more efficient to get a particular profit level out of the lowest possible sales turnover. High turnover at low margins usually implies higher working capital levels, more debtors, some of which will go bad, more work for more people and therefore higher direct and indirect costs and expenses. None of these is essential to the attainment of the specified objectives.

Better marketing

The objectives specified are fairly simple, but the means of converting them into action is not always fully understood.

This section is about maximising the volume and quality of customer contacts. This means attracting more, converting more, satisfying more and making better contacts. But how? There are several routes. The first involves improving your contact with existing customers by:

(a) doing the previous job properly;
(b) ensuring that they understand the previous job was done properly;
(c) getting more data about them and their needs;
(d) asking them for more business;
(e) asking them to introduce new customers;
(f) occasionally reminding them that you exist;
(g) offering them renewed service, from time to time;
(h) offering them a different service.

The second route to better marketing demands that you do substantially the same with known potential customers who have not yet used your services.

The third involves identifying and making contact with new potential customers through referrals and research, followed by direct marketing efforts. The fourth? Probably converting into sales more of the enquiries which result from your past and current marketing efforts, and in particular being equipped to respond properly to cold approaches from new contacts of this kind. Some businesses can be remarkably hostile or cool to potential customers whose sudden appearance takes them by surprise. This applies equally at reception and board level.

The fifth route is easy – and important: doing the current work better. The sixth is difficult and often forgotten: ensuring the customer understands that the current job has been done well is as important as actually doing it well, though without the latter, the former may be wholly wasted.

Seventh, rejecting marginal businesses. This is difficult but worthwhile in the long run. If there is something about the particular customer's business which makes it unlikely to be profitable for you or if the service cannot be delivered to the satisfaction of the customer, you must seek either to make it viable or to reject it. Making a mess of the work and making a loss are both unacceptable, unless the loss is a loss leader which will secure extra business later. The latter situation is rare: usually it will be taken as a precedent and you will be expected to do future work at the same low price.

Eighth, asking for the next job or for a recommendation. Ninth, carrying out research to identify what sort of customer and work constitutes *better* business in your field. There are several possibilities. Better business may include:

(a) work which can be done quicker or cheaper at the same price;
(b) work which commands a premium price;
(c) customers who pay better;
(d) customers who are more likely to come back quickly;
(e) work with high visibility, so that new customers can see you in the act;
(f) work that expands the market, i.e. for people who have not previously used such a service.

Tenth, turning all lukewarm contacts, social and professional, into customers or potential customers by ensuring they know what you do and giving them a means of finding you again.

At this point it is worth stressing that most of the above courses of action require very little expenditure. Many of them can be done as part of your existing employees' daily work, and may even save them work. The rest is largely low cost effort. Better still, because a clearer understanding of the marketing implications of their work will enhance employees' self-esteem and motivation, the general quality and direction of their work should improve.

It should also be evident that the various routes towards the company's objectives described above involve several features which can improve profit without increasing turnover. Better gross margins, achieved by lower unit costs or higher unit prices, have great merits. Better net profits, achieved with lower overheads, fewer bad debts or better payment patterns, can also avoid the need for increasing turnover.

This is not to decry volume growth, but volume growth with

static or reduced margins can be a fool's paradise. In any organisation there will always be somebody on the sales side who is obsessed with turnover growth at all costs, and is prepared to do a deal which may appear marginally profitable but, when the semi-variable expenses have been taken into account, is in fact at or below breakeven point. Semi-variable expenses, in the accountant's definition, are ones which tend to vary to some extent, but not completely, with extra volume.

Three important facts, which even some accountants do not know and others prefer to ignore, are as follows:

- many fixed expenses are in fact semi-variable;
- most semi-variables vary more than you expect; and
- some variables vary *less* than you had planned.

It follows that if you rely too much on the variability or otherwise of costs and expenses in deciding whether your prices actually generate a profit, you can be in for a nasty shock. Another truth about variances from the norm (or standard) is that most variances tend to be adverse, i.e. there are more things which can go gratuitously wrong than things which can go gratuitously right. The concept of 'windfall profits' has been around for quite a while, to describe the unexpected favourable variance. The accountancy profession has been remarkably coy about recognising that the 'windfall loss' is equally credible – and more frequent in practice.

The enemy within

If the marketing effort is to be productive, everyone on your staff must contribute. It is not enough that they avoid negative marketing. They must also be positively educated about their role as 'marketing staff'. It is essential to avoid the 'misinformation vacuum'.

The first stage in the educational process is the definition and promulgation of your corporate objectives. Very few companies bother to do this, so you will steal a march on the opposition. Employees who actually know what the organisation is doing, and why, have a distinct advantage over those who do not.

The next stage is to specify *personal* tasks and objectives, and to link them clearly with the corporate goals already described.

The third stage involves skills training. Broadly, the company has an obligation to train people in the practical skills relevant to their jobs. These skills, when taught, tend to be the mechanical ones associated with the tasks of a job, not with the corporate objectives, so for example, receptionists will receive visitors and typists will type, but none of them will be taught about the marketing content of their jobs. They will perform their jobs much better if these skills are coupled with a positive attitude to corporate needs and an awareness of marketing as a route to the corporate ends.

In this context, it is useful to remember the saying, 'If you're not with us, you're against us'. There is no middle ground. Customers and potential customers do not want aggression, either on the telephone, by letter or face to face. They want someone who seems to be on their side. Neutrality and apathy are not enough: in fact, they are the enemies of good customer relations. If they exist in your organisation it is not the fault of the perpetrators, but of the management.

(a) If the perpetrators are ignorant, the management should have arranged for them to be trained and/or educated (skills training and knowledge are two different things, but they both have to be provided by the management).

(b) If the management has provided training or educational input but the employees are not competent to receive or apply it, the employees have been either recruited or promoted wrongly – again, a management failure.

(c) If the perpetrators are competent and well briefed, any failure must be due to stress, lack of motivation or overwork. Yet again, the management is probably to blame.

Monitor and support

The final stage in the educational process is another area in which the management often fails. It involves monitoring and supporting employees. Most managements are reactive: they will criticise major faults and, less often, praise excellence. Relatively few managers discipline themselves to keep an eye on their subordinates' mainstream activities. Too often delegation breeds abdication of responsibility and, if there are no crises, the 'no news is good news' principle applies. Harassed managers do not go out looking for trouble. 'Looking for trouble' is not the solution, but a tactful low key review, to ensure that subordinates have not deviated from positive action, is always worthwhile.

If employees are not given clear directions, the mistakes which are made will have a serious cumulative effect. For example, sending relatively urgent documents second class rather than first loses more than a couple of days in transit. A full week or a full month may slip in the cycle of affairs at the other end. Worse, it may lose a contract, delay payments due, or convince a potential client that your reputation for speed and excellence is a fiction.

Failure to follow the correct telephone answering formula may leave a potential or existing customer with the impression that his or her name, number and message have been conveyed to someone for action, when this has not, in fact, happened.

Failure to switch on the answering machine at night may confuse and upset a key customer who has become used to phoning in vital requests out of hours.

Sending out certain documents on plain paper rather than headed may, in some sectors, breach the law; in others it may invalidate the contractual obligation; and in others it may mean that the honest customer cannot pay you.

Omitting enclosures from marketing mailings or including the wrong ones, may have a less compelling effect than was intended on particular recipients or even be completely irrelevant to their carefully researched needs.

Mechanistic credit control without regard to the operational customer relationship is often a reason for lost business.

Thoughtless explanations when managers cannot come to the telephone may be misunderstood. An employee who says 'He's not back from lunch yet' at three o'clock gives the wrong impression of someone who may be travelling back from an extremely short, sober, lunch with a customer 30 miles away. Even if the lunch is long, local, boozy and not with a customer, it is a tactless excuse. In either case, 'He's with a customer and we expect him back shortly' is the better formula.

Similarly, 'He's busy' is not a tactful way of refusing to connect a caller. A good excuse is, 'He's interviewing and we try not to disturb him during interviews, but he'll be free in half an hour.' If this is inappropriate in your business, there must be an equally respectable excuse which allows you to give precedence to people present in person, over telephone intruders.

People

The conventional wisdom is that most people can do better if they are better motivated and directed (*see* Robert Townsend's *Up the Organisation* and Sir Michael Edwardes' *Back From The Brink*). It should be added that your staff must meet certain minimum standards in the first place. If they do not, it is unlikely they will ever achieve excellence – or even an above-average performance.

Time and effort spent in converting poor performers into average performers may be well spent, as a short-term expedient. However, the medium-term solution must be to promote or recruit people capable of producing an above-average performance. The old school sales rep was unlikely to be a graduate – or of particularly high intelligence. The new demands of the sales role, including an understanding of marketing and a conceptual grasp of the customers' objectives, make it important that you appoint people with the personality and aptitude to match. Better recruitment and/or internal appointments, based on an objective measurement of the job requirements and the individual, will enable you to fulfil your corporate objectives most successfully.

3   The numbers game

Variables are often taken for granted or unrecognised ...

Relatively small improvements at each stage of marketing can achieve dramatic changes in the overall effect of your efforts.

It is convenient to illustrate this with a direct mail example, because the availability of statistics gives us a firm base from which to project the results of the improvements. Other areas of marketing are less easily researched.

There are some direct mail exponents who get by on a response rate of one to three per cent. For convenience, let us start with the one per cent operators who, it must be said are tolerably happy with the results (though complacent may be the better description).

Direct mail is a useful test because in many cases it is necessary to take the potential customer from unawareness to awareness, to comprehension, to conviction and to action with just one set of papers. Unless there is some wider parallel marketing effort going on, the mailshot stands or falls on its own merits.

There are several areas in which decisions must be made about a direct mail shot, as follows:

(a) Target;
(b) Timing;
(c) Product (what service are you going to offer, at what price?);
(d) Medium;
(e) Message.

Target

- People of the right sex and age at their home addresses may seem like a suitable target. Sometimes this is not enough and it is vital that they are also householders.
- An up-to-date list of computer managers may sound relevant – but are they running the right hardware?
- Sometimes the list, as defined, sounds perfect. But when was it compiled?
- Chartered accountants in practice, in the right geographical area, may be relevant to your service, but why not focus on those of the right age, to improve the chances that they are young enough (or senior enough, depending on your product) to be preferred targets.

All the above improvements to your list are feasible from desk research. Better still, a discussion with a good proprietary list broker can identify lists of people who have actually bought products and services which you perceive as comparable with your own.

The principle of identifying the target accurately and modifying the marketing strategy accordingly applies equally to advertising. In 1987 I researched the costs of reaching key people in a profession whose members were concentrated in the West End of London and, to a lesser extent, the City. Advertising in the national media was out: too expensive. The same applied to the trade press, in view of the space and media needed to make an adequate impact for what had to be a short, low-budget campaign. Research finally indicated that we could do it most cheaply and quite effectively by putting black and white posters on selected bus shelters (the Adshel concept) near the head offices of the target companies. Sneaky but effective.

Note that *all* the above mail examples imply a substantial multiplication effect. Moving from a five per cent to a 25% response rate is a 400% improvement.

Timing

Some services are not susceptible to precise advance warning: they may cater for needs which arise unexpectedly and unpredictably.

However, some control is possible. There are discretionary services which do badly when people are concentrating on Christmas shopping, January sales and holidays. Wedding-linked services can be targeted from the engagements column. Baby products, less effectively, from past weddings. Some services can be sold to companies whose corporate relocation or development is mentioned in the trade press. Offers to help small businessmen with their VAT may work best around each month end when one-third of all businesses are certainly having their quarterly panic. The examples will be different for your service, but research or lateral thinking should produce some improvement. Avoiding the wasted half of the year, month, or quarter may double your efficiency.

Product

Here changes may be more difficult to effect. Sometimes, in a service business, you cannot change the nature of the product. If you unblock drains, clean windows, perform audits or repair burst pipes, the core service is fairly rigidly defined.

However, there are variables. Customers' perception of the offering can be changed. The price can be significant: terms of business, warranties, comfort factors, the convenience of your location, can all help. The offer you make is not necessarily identical with that of your competitors. For example, in some cases, stating the price or making the point that it is the cheapest available may be a unique selling proposition (USP). In others the warranty can help. Dyno-Rod offered 'satisfaction – or your blockage back'. Not quite the conventional warranty, but a brilliant way of reminding people of the benefits.

Terms matter too. Stage payments, credit, 'Send no money now' or even '*Do* send money now because we can't do it this cheaply otherwise' all help. Not so easy to do with a service, but perhaps we can turn this to advantage. Can you offer an image of reliability ('Boringly reliable', as in the Minolta product offering) or certainty, which the opposition cannot? The trouble with a service offering is that the consumers cannot get their hands on it. The fact that they have to pay for it before seeing the results is another disadvantage. Any

19

reassurance you can offer gives you extra credibility. Even the things you take for granted may be USPs.

In my own selection company we were racking our brains to find something unique about us which we could mention to potential customers. We decided to do a little research (time spent in reconnaissance is seldom wasted) and found to our surprise that the things we regarded as the common core of our own and our competitors' offering were in fact rare but in demand. For example, the fact that we:

- always produced a shortlist of candidates for the client company;
- delivered it on time; and
- included in it people who met the client's specifications

were actually unusual and worth mentioning. 'Boringly reliable' has a wider application, including perhaps the things you do well but take for granted.

Medium

'Direct mail' may appear to define the medium. Not so. It only specifies that the package goes by post. The nature of that package is very much at your discretion. This is a good example of the variables which are often taken for granted or unrecognised, so they are listed in detail.

- First or second class post, or a false telegram?
- Envelope, package, postcard or airmail letter?
- Plain outer, coloured, bulky or thin?
- Contents: one sheet?
            several?
            several, including piggy-backs?
            brochure(s) and letter?
            gift? gimmick? grabber?

- Typography? Young people often devise texts which middle-aged targets cannot read.

There are many consumers, business and personal, who have prejudices about direct mail. Some love false telegrams: some junk them. Some throw away unopened envelopes which betray the contents. Few will junk a bulky packet. Few can resist recorded delivery. Several offers are more likely to succeed than one (so piggy-back more widely, to jointly-relevant targets).

There is frequently an emotional barrier about piggy-backing. Lots of marketing people, entrepreneurs and sales managers feel insecure about putting their messages in the same envelope as messages from other companies. This is understandable. If it is done badly – for example a new liqueur is advertised with a new gin palace, a downmarket hotel, sex aids, motor caravans, liver transplants and a health farm – one or more of the organisations might rightly feel that its image was being frayed at the edges by association.

Alternatively, if a piggy-back mailing included Rolls Royce, Bickerton bicycles, the best of Japanese cameras, the best shotguns in the UK and a really smooth malt whisky, the participants might feel comfortable. So might the target customers. If your service is in that league, great. If not, find a reliable plebian set of products and services to piggy-back with. Correct associations *always* enhance provided the rest of the variables are handled properly.

Message

There are three key things which can usually be improved in direct mail messages. The personalisation is one. The nature of the offer (not usually dependent on the product) is next. The request for action is third, but crucial.

Making the recipient feel the message is personal to him or her is a cardinal rule. Apart from anything else, this helps to ensure the text is not filtered out or thrown away by a secretary.

Offering something of interest to *them*, not just of interest to *you*, is also vital. Your USP must be evident.

Asking them to do something about it is also an essential part of the process. Few direct mailshots which I receive fully satisfy these three simple criteria.

The message should also tell them who and where you are. Sometimes it is enough to issue a description of the service and a telephone number, but other people buying high-value services probably want to know where you are, whether you are a limited company and the name of the person to deal with. Most research in this area suggests that the boss should sign the letter for best effect.

Getting all these right can enhance your conversion ratio quite dramatically, but there are two further ingredients which must be linked in.

'Response medium'

'Reply instructions' might be a better phrase. If you have got as far as tempting people to respond, making it easy for them to do so surely makes sense. It may be that your preferred response route is not theirs. You can choose whether they reply by telephone, letter, coupon, telex, Micronet or carrier pigeon (don't laugh – it's been tried, and it worked), but if you *prevent* them using alternative routes you may lose sales. You decide, but let it be a decision and not an omission.

Your reaction

Following all the suggestions outlined above is no use, however, if your staff are not programmed to respond correctly. If, at the end of the chain, you fail to convert a live enquiry into a sale – perhaps the caller's address or telephone number were not recorded by someone who did not know how the offer was to be handled – you do not just throw away one target, you also throw away all the effort which surrounded it, i.e. the redundant mailings which were designed to elicit that one valid response.

4 Win/win

Youth is mostly about making errors you can later learn from . . .

It is a basic technique of the sales professional to offer the customer two buying options. Instead of asking for a yes/no decision about buying, the competent sales rep always offers a choice between two different products or two different ways of buying the same product. This simple concept is sometimes forgotten by marketing experts and often unknown to amateurs, yet it is an essential ingredient in the process of turning a contact into a sale. The win/win choice is so much more useful than a win/lose possibility that it seems the only natural way to proceed, but in practice it has to be remembered and applied by rote until it really does become natural. Look at the efforts of your marketing department and there is a good chance that the lesson has been ignored in preparing some or all of your existing marketing literature. These omissions constitute gratuitous error.

AGE

AGE, in this context, is a mnemonic for Avoiding Gratuitous Error. With luck or an open mind you learn this with the advancing years, through experience. Youth is mostly about making errors you can later learn from.

An example may help. There is a deep-seated need in marketing staff to be seen to be doing something. Even those who have read good books or seen the videos about time management and thus know that it is good practice to sit and think, still feel guilty about being seen to do so, perhaps by people who have not absorbed the principle. The result, particularly for people who believe that the best is the enemy of the good, is that they do something just to avoid being observed doing nothing. That something is often not just not best, but not good either.

Time management also tempts people to say, 'We must get the mailshot/ad/newsletter out on time.' Unfortunately, if the delay is in the message-building part of the creative process, imposing such a time limit may mean that you issue a message which is sub-standard, ineffective or even counter-productive (*see* Chapter 1, *Negative marketing*). My company once dealt with a problem like this when we introduced a queueing system for the monthly direct mailshot. The consultant who staked the first claim got the earliest shot. The catch was that the claim had to be made by showing a message or package which was genuinely worth sending. Only when this test had been passed was there any question of a place in the queue.

This is, of course, a counsel of perfection. There are some businesses where the marketing department has to keep issuing messages to its target market so that by the law of averages it ensures that at least some of them buy the product next week or next month. This sort of treadmill militates against best practice and is the ideal breeding ground for gratuitous error.

The need to deliver messages on time is a powerful argument for tolerating mediocrity or worse. But it need not be. If someone running such a project thought harder about the problem, it should become apparent that time management does not in itself demand a pot-boiler every month. True time management permits you to say, 'OK, let's recognise that we may have to do January in the same old way, but if we start February *now* it can be done with a little more forethought, and March can be excellent.' Lateral thinking would permit you to buy even more time by making January's effort a quick re-hash of last year's most effective effort, so that you could concentrate more resources on February, March, April and so on. You would also have an interesting benchmark for later results analysis. If you have not been analysing results, now is the time to start. The example may look oversimplified but it is real. There is probably a parallel in your own organisation.

Keeping customers

It was stressed earlier that one of the most powerful things you can do in marketing is to make the current customers happy. This goes some way towards ensuring that they will use you again and/or recommend you. It does not go all the way. In many cases customers will have to be reminded or encouraged. The nature of this retention marketing inevitably varies with the value of, and frequency of need for, the service but on a basic level, you ask them to come back. If, for your sort of service, this is too brash, at least say that you will be pleased to help them again. Many service businesses fail to ask and are then surprised and aggrieved when the customers go elsewhere. If in doubt, ask, not least because the customers may be pleased that you still want them.

Beyond this, there are several variables which affect the ways in which you try to keep customers. First, low-value services with no need for early repetition deserve a relatively simple message. Ask them to remember and recommend you, and give them some way of doing so. A business card might do: two would be better. An item whose intrinsic merits demand retention is better still, for example, next year's calendar, with your name and trade on it. Alas, cost dictates that you cannot do much more for low-value services – unless you have other services you should be mentioning.

Low–value services which can be repetitive offer much more scope. The points above apply as a minimum, but there are several low-cost measures you can take as well. A 'season-ticket' approach may be possible, i.e. some form of discount for volume. A swimming pool might offer blocks of tickets at a reduced rate. In inflationary times you could offer to hold this year's price for next year, to existing customers.

One mail order photo processor has a brilliant technique. They give credits for exposures that do not come out, to be used against the next film order you send in. So do their competitors. What their competitors have not yet realised is that the laboratory in question generates massive customer loyalty by including a credit voucher for one or two exposures 'lost' even when the customer has a full batch of perfect prints. Most customers do not notice or think they have been lucky. I only noticed this because I regularly sneak 25 or more exposures onto a 24–shot film, and was intrigued when the credit vouchers still kept flowing. This wanton distribution of negotiable paper may sound unwise, but it is only money's worth when the repeat purchase occurs, and at that moment it becomes a very small price for the repeat sale.

The next challenge is the high-value recurring service. If the value includes a substantial gross margin over and above the variable cost, there are massive opportunities for carrying out all the above suggestions and adding to them. However, remember that you seek to influence the customer both as repeat purchaser and as influencer of others. Good direct mail may help. Small gifts which remind them of you and thank them can also be appropriate. Enhanced service may work, i.e. some form of preferred customers' privileges which gives them priority, free extras (nearly always better than discounting the base price), or perhaps credit facilities.

Finally, the needs of a high-value, non-recurring service. This is a major problem but, because of the high value, one worth tackling. It is obvious that if a service engineer has installed in a home a fixture of which the average home needs only one, or an undertaker has buried one of your ancestors and you do not have a ready supply of ailing relatives, the chances of a repeat purchase are slim. Fortunately, there are several things which can be done:

(a) sell a different service;
(b) sell the same service for the second home (second home owners are by definition likely to be key customers for many high-value services), or for the office;
(c) sell for the home something the customer has tried in the office; or
(d) offer a worthwhile incentive for introducing new customers (ideally something with large retail margins so the customer thinks that the value is greater than the wholesale cost to you). Even offer them money – if your gross margins are good enough.

Finally, never forget that good service, perceived as such, is half the battle. The higher the value of your service the more important this is, and the more chance you have of allocating funds to cement the relationship for the future. Often it does not even require funds. For example, auditors nowadays always send clients an annual 'management letter' which details control and systems weaknesses identified. These tend to be couched in fairly negative terms. Those which instead indicate the profit effect of curing the faults, or even suggest constructive action unrelated to past faults, look very good by comparison with the rest. A letter which offers savings in excess of the audit fee makes the audit look free, even if you do not adopt the suggestions. Many service advisers could do the same.

5   The product

The packaging surrounding the service may be just as important as the service itself . . .

The product is service

But what is the service? Because the results of the service are generally not visible to enough potential customers, there is room for confusion about the nature of the service.

You must know what the service is before you can market it effectively. This may sound like a truism but there are three different 'truths' about many products and most services. These are:

● what the product or service really is;
● what the vendor 'knows' it is; and
● what the buyers 'know' it is.

There is perhaps a fourth: what the non-buyers know it is, which may or may not coincide with the buyers' view. Perhaps that is why they are not buyers. The three primary truths do not necessarily coincide, and if you are selling a service it is desperately important that you recognise this possibility. If you do not, you may:

● price the service wrongly;
● package it wrongly;
● select the wrong target market;
● market badly; or
● operate inefficiently.

Fortunately, one truth is likely to be common to most services. 'What it really is' nearly always involves the sale of time, which may be in the form of labour-hours, machine-hours, other asset/space hours or a mixture of these. Usually the vendors recognise this, as they have to pay for the people, machines and other assets involved.

The problem comes because the buyers seldom see it that way. They may recognise a connection, but to them the product is *service*, not time. Their expectation relates to the results of the service, even though the way the time is spent may condition their appreciation. In other words the packaging surrounding the service may be just as important as the service itself. This makes it doubly important to know what your USP is. People may come initially for one reason, but return for a different one.

How is your service perceived in comparison with the rest? It may succeed because it is:

available now	honest
authoritative	market leader
better	needed
cheaper	prestigious
different	personal
dedicated	recommended
expensive	reliable
enjoyable	supportive
faster	trustworthy
fashionable	unhurried
good value	unique
guaranteed	versatile
high quality	

However, the customers may come back for different reasons – because they perceive your staff as adding something special to the service. That something could be crucial to the buying decision. For instance, it may be very important that they are perceived as:

attentive	punctual
considerate	professional
cheerful	respectful
chatty (or not)	reassuring

competent	relaxed
friendly	straightforward
knowledgeable	young
mature	

People of all ages and sexes use personal services or stop using them – often for superficial reasons. I cannot bear chatty hairdressers, whether or not they try to sell hair restorer. My wife cannot bear hairdressers who ignore her. The quality of the service takes second place to its 'packaging', if the buyer has a choice.

This applies to business services too. Major firms in some professions are now used to the possibility that they will have to present their services against competitors for major new accounts. The process is disparagingly known as a 'beauty parade' but the firms tend to prepare as if the assessment were being made on an objective basis, whereas in many cases the client's feeling of empathy with the presenting team is the deciding factor. The same empathy may preserve such a relationship through later adverse circumstances, so perhaps the subjective basis of choice is actually valid. It is useful to remember this when considering the problems and opportunities which arise from the different perceptions of your service.

The first and most crucial point has already been mentioned. The core of the service is likely to be chargeable time, but the perceptions relate to results. You can do one of three things about this:

(a) educate buyers about the value of the time spent;
(b) deliver the expected results, with or without educating the buyers; or
(c) work more quickly, so that results can be achieved with less expenditure of time and there is less need to justify time-related charges.

Option (c) has great merits, because it permits you to take competitive pricing action or to leave prices unchanged and enhance your margins. It also reinforces the point that what you are actually selling is a combination of experience, skill and time, not just time.

The second point is that if buyers expect something which

you do not or cannot deliver they are going to be disappointed. Your marketing must address itself to:

(a) changing the service, if appropriate; or
(b) changing the perception.

It is absolutely vital that this problem be solved in one way or the other, or your marketing effort is going to be partially or wholly irrelevant, if not counter-productive. Equally, repeat purchases, normally a substantial source of your core business, may be eroded or eliminated. It is always depressing when a new customer, who should be a cause for celebration, quickly becomes an ex-customer. When this happens for avoidable reasons, it constitutes self-inflicted injury.

Finding out what customers and potential customers think is very important in this and other contexts. It need not be expensive. Most businesses do not listen to their customers enough. Many are afraid to ask for their reactions, for fear of being told something they do not like, or provoking the customer into thinking something adverse. This head-in-sand attitude offers no scope for improvement.

The research starts with a brief to staff to listen to what is volunteered by existing and potential customers. The next step is to go out and ask. Surveys are seductive. People like answering them if they are not too difficult to complete and they are offered something in return (e.g. the survey results, a better service or a voucher against future services).

In most cases, this should be enough. If not, it may not be necessary to spend tens of thousand on full-scale market research. The next source of research is the local business studies network. Mature marketing students at business schools and technical colleges are always looking for projects. They come without built-in overheads and may be very cost-effective when unleashed on a research project. They may also be a useful sounding board about marketing in general.

There is an additional bonus about finding out what customers really want out of you. Not only can you adjust the service to fit their needs, you may also be able to omit ingredients they do not need or actively dislike. This can save costs, time and customers.

It is not acceptable to assume that you must be doing it right already, just because there appear to be enough customers. This assumption is dangerous because it ignores all the opportunities specified or implied above, and obscures one extra potential problem: if your assumptions about the product and your customers' needs are not valid, you may not understand the warning signs before a market change breaks the existing link between customers and service. Worse, if you do not know what the real link was, you may find it difficult or impossible to rebuild it or devise a viable alternative.

Find out *now* what the service really is, what the customers are buying and what they really want. Armed with this knowledge you can enhance the key characteristics – and flaunt them! Your business may depend on it.

The service as product

Another opportunity arises if we reconsider those features which were dismissed earlier as irrelevant to a service business. Production, warehousing and purchase of materials probably remain outside our needs, but there are several ingredients in the product-oriented business which we can plagiarise. For example, quality control, packaging, warranty, delivery specifications and brochures. This section is about treating a service like a product, how to do it, and why.

The 'why' comes first. Products have something to teach us. Because they exist they *demand* that we do certain things with them and their physical existence makes it easier or unnecessary to be disciplined about presenting them accurately. In a service business, the simple point about specifying clearly what the service is can often be forgotten because, like a product, everyone 'knows' what it is. For example: if we return to the inventor of the better mousetrap, it is evident that the existence of his product and its operation made it unnecessary to specify the product in detail except for the benefit of the production team. If, however, he had invented a service, he would have been well advised to put the essentials down on paper, for three reasons:

(a) employees do not usually know what the service really is until they are told;

(b) they cannot tell the customers until they know;
(c) the customers have erroneous preconceptions.

Just as gossip, rumour and speculation fill every information vacuum, so do employees with initiative invent and disseminate their own views of the service unless the vacuum is replaced by solid information.

This leads to two horrible, avoidable problems. I became aware of the first many years ago when I overheard a secretary with initiative describing our service to a potential client. Her discourse drew on her extensive experience, elsewhere, of the management selection business. It was fluent; it was clear; it was convincing. It was also diametrically opposed to everything that we were trying to do to set outselves apart from the opposition.

This was not good, but it was our fault and it was fairly readily curable. The real disasters occurred several years later when it became apparent that, in spite of verbal briefings during induction, exposure to best practice ('sitting with Nellie') and access to all our client literature, I had hired three consultants in succession dedicated to providing their view of the service rather than our product offering. This became evident quite quickly with two of the consultants, because their operational performance never achieved even average levels. The third almost succeeded in spite of the deviations and therefore remained undetected longer, but with greater long-term damage to the image we were trying to project. Clear step-by-step codification of the service would have prevented this. It would also have provided a better foundation for the client brochures, both as to the content of the service and the likely results.

Quality control

Clear specifications permit better objective-setting and the opportunity for some form of quality control, which will differ dramatically from service to service but can usually be tested by asking this sort of question in the closing stages:

● does the customer (dog, carpet, paperwork, etc.) look better?

33

- is the garment (plumbing, car, customer) undamaged?
- is the subject of the service improved?
- does the customer feel satisfied?

Customer satisfaction is not the only criterion, but it is a big one. That is why the way you package your service counts. And the way you tidy up afterwards.

Packaging

The consumer who opens a stout box, lovingly packed, and lifts out a pristine object wrapped in a durable waterproof plastic shrinkwrap, is likely to have a better image of the product than if it is hidden in crumpled up pages of newspaper and still bears traces of greasy fingerprints. 'Tidying up afterwards', with broom or letter, is the equivalent. Even in accountancy, head-hunting, law and medicine you tidy up afterwards. The need is not confined to chimney cleaning and plumbing.

There is also potential for packaging, earlier in the process. This may include:

(a) the way you present paperwork from a professional office – binders and folders rather than naked letters and texts;
(b) the appearance of instructions, guarantee and, as mentioned above, the specification of the service – all these add credibility;
(c) a livery for the employees and vehicles providing the service. It should be self-evident that a smart employee with some visible identification, in a matching vehicle, looks more convincing than a scruffy anonymous one in a rusty van. Even the professions and the skilled trades benefit from this policy: house ties, gold embossing on briefcase, discreet nametags, company logos on work folders all help. And lift self-esteem.

Warranty

This is not part of the packaging, although the documentary evidence of warranty may be. Formal, clear, helpful warranties have several advantages. For instance:

(a) a clear, informative text is good for your image:
(b) intelligible instructions may help people claim properly – or realise they cannot reasonably claim, without feeling cheated;
(c) they may limit your liability to a reasonable level.

Delivery

Although delivery may seem to belong to a product-based business, it may in fact be even more important in the service context. If your customer needs a *product* at 9 a.m. on Friday 13th, it is almost always acceptable to deliver it on the afternoon of Thursday 12th. It will still be there at the right time, unless very perishable.

If the *service* is needed at 9 a.m. on Friday, being there on the wrong day is much less likely to be acceptable. The relevant people may not be there or the object to be serviced may not be ready, or even present. (This is even worse if the customer is coming to you.)

Time management is more important with services than with products. Delivery is a crucial example. This is particularly true of high-value professional services where you are delivering chargeable time and experience, the delivery of which involves two-way communication. Some professionals consistently manage their time badly and forget that every time they re-shuffle their diaries, they waste either their employees' or their clients' time, and lose goodwill.

There are lessons for all kinds of services here. Members of learned professions cannot afford unprofessional time management. Reliable tradesmen stand out like a shining light among their unreliable competitors. (Eventually, even the nationalised industries and private monopolies may realise this.)

6   The price

The price of all services is always wrong . . .

The price of your service is wrong. The price of all services is always wrong. There is no one right price, even if it is set by custom, law or the rules of a trade association or professional body. Even with a fixed price, payment terms can change the effective cost to the consumer.

Price is one of the variables which affect consumers' perceptions of the service. Price is itself conditioned by your costs, expenses, capacity, preferred volume, planned margins and desired profits, but no one of these and no combination can dictate a theoretically perfect price. Experts talk about markets being price sensitive. It is true that people and companies are influenced by price, but not in a way which would permit one to draw a formal and precise curve plotting sales volume against different levels of price. There are several reasons for this. The most obvious are set out below.

(a) Some people buy without knowing the price.
(b) Some people buy because the product is expensive, others because it is cheap. (The same product may be perceived as expensive by one consumer, cheap by another.)
(c) Some people buy regardless of the price.
(d) Repeat purchasers in particular are likely to buy on factors other than price.
(e) Good marketing can make the price less important or wholly unimportant.

(f) If you price precisely against a direct competitor you ensure that the buying decision is made on factors other than price.

This leads us to several interesting propositions, as follows.

(a) There is no point in being cheapest:

- if nobody knows you are cheapest;
- if many buyers do not care;
- if enough buyers want 'the best' and actually assume the most expensive is best;
- if your service is at least on a par with the competition or can be perceived as better;
- if you are running into insuperable capacity problems at your present volume;
- just because you have wholly or partially ignored over-heads in computing your price;
- because you undervalue the market price of your own service;
- except as part of a coherent marketing strategy.

(b) There is therefore a case for pricing firmly so that you have some leeway for:

- special offers, cash discounts, bad debts;
- price reduction if the demand does not respond to other marketing efforts;
- repeat purchase (or introduction) incentives to past and current buyers;
- adverse cost movements.

(c) Even with labour-intensive services, the price is likely to be at least double the direct costs (to cover overheads) so that you have considerable scope for marginal pricing in the short term, while you are experimenting with your marketing and pricing.

With services which are not labour intensive, the scope is even wider as the variable costs of providing the service are generally even lower in proportion to the market price.

This is not an argument for permanent marginal pricing, but it does mean that you can make individual or short-term bulk pricing decisions with greater flexibility, provided there is a legitimate commercial reason for doing so. Such reasons might include:

- the likelihood of later repeat business at full price (an introductory offer, for example);
- the existence of a core business which, at full price, already fully recovers all overheads for the period in question;
- a need to keep the employees occupied or to pay their wages rather than laying them off;
- cash flow, particularly if you can collect sales revenue before you have to pay costs and expenses.

(d) No price is absolute. Your payment structure, collection terms, the way you implement those terms and any financial warranty all fine-tune the price. This flexibility can be used in several ways:

- tough payment terms can make your reasonable price yield more than a competitor's softly collected but apparently equal or higher price;
- a sympathetically structured price can help close the sale;
- front-end loading can help your cash flow.

Do not be too keen to introduce back-end loading, stage payments or any other form of deferred terms without the machinery (post-dated cheques, standing orders, direct debits) to ensure payment on time. Debts become less real to the debtor as time passes and they do not improve if you are soft about collection.

All overdue debts are doubtful. Nearly all bad debts were doubtful before they were bad. Bad debts do not just cost the price of one sale, they cost the profit on several. Avoid them, by early action, which starts with clear terms of business and a clear understanding in the customers' minds of the true worth of your services. There is no point in getting the price right if you do not then collect the cash.

To sum up, remember that the price is part of the product specification but a part which is quite easily altered or packaged differently.

Sensitive attention to pricing can have a dramatic effect on volumes, gross revenues, gross margins and net profits, sometimes without the customer really noticing. Apathy or insensitive attention to pricing can also have dramatic effects – this time negative ones.

Pitching your price

A compelling reason for not being too cheap is that hardly anybody wants to start negotiating *upwards* from the declared price list. (If you do encounter this phenomenon, be suspicious).

Product manufacturers prefer to declare a maximum price, perhaps the 'recommended retail' price, from which they discount more or less heavily according to the nature of the product and the negotiating tactics of the particular purchase. Those vendors who work from a declared 'wholesale' price list are at an immediate disadvantage because the more powerful wholesalers are always able to trim something off even these levels.

In a service business the formal price list is less common but the principle remains valid. If you believe the buyer to be price sensitive and give a discount in the first price you quote, there is nowhere to go but further down when they start negotiating. It is probably better to mention the highest gross price you can, and in the same breath offer a lower price but one which is still well *above* your real target. They can then chip away at the discounted level, while you seek a trade-off in return for each step of your retreat.

The trade-offs will depend very much on the nature of your business, but there is ample scope. For instance, you may choose to dictate:

- which currency you get paid in;
- earlier payment terms;
- timing of the service at *your* convenience, not theirs;
- adjustment to the service to reduce your costs.

We cannot stress too strongly the importance of a trade-off against each concession. Not only does it improve the terms of business for you, it also has two key side-effects.

- The buyers feel more satisfied with the deal. If you give way completely they will have a nagging feeling that they could have got more.
- They may stop trying to push the price down sooner than if you were retreating fast.

One of the dictums of this book is that the price should not be seen as a key issue, but it would be naive to ignore its existence altogether!

Barter

Finally, a word or two on the ultimate in non-monetary pricing.

North of the equator, barter is most frequently found in trade between the West and Iron Curtain countries, to compensate for a shortage of foreign exchange or to shift products which might not be sold on merit. However, it has special advantages in dealings between service companies and there is a good case for exploring barter deals both with suppliers and potential customers, to turn one into the other.

The key reason for recommending this to service-based companies is that all except labour-intensive services should have generous gross margins. This gives you the chance to offer something with a high perceived value and a low direct cost, to firms whose services have the same characteristics. The result can be viewed in two ways.

At best you get incremental sales, in exchange for a service you would have bought there or elsewhere at full price. At worst, the service you might or might not have bought from them only costs you the variable costs of your bartered service. There are related advantages. Turning customers into suppliers, and vice-versa, cements relationships and can yield partial or total exclusivity. It may, in some cases, expand the market. Properly done, it looks professional and can be presented as showing a proper concern for others' commercial interests and objectives. They too should perceive incremental sales and/or reduced costs at their end.

None of the above is an absolute argument for barter deals, but the opportunity of expanding market penetration and reducing selling costs and marketing expenses must be quite attractive to many service businesses. Just the fact that you mention it to potential cross traders may give them a warm glow about you, whether they take up the offer or not. People who *sell* high-value services are still mean about *buying* them, and the accountants, solicitors, consultants and software experts who whistle incredulously at each others' bills might be particularly susceptible to this concept.

7   Managing your markets

Even the most rigid market can be expanded ...

This chapter is about some mistaken attitudes to target markets; it contains several conventional solutions and a few unconventional opportunities.

The problem attitudes can be reduced to four, which are summarised below.

- Of course we know our markets – look how well we are selling.
- We do not need to investigate our markets – look how well we are selling.
- We do not know what our targets are but we have supreme confidence in the product/service.
- We know our market because we researched it and we are happy with the results.

All these are dangerous. The first three are easiest to criticise because they all depend on the status quo. They will get a nasty shock and be unprepared to take corrective action when the market, whatever it is, goes bad.

The fourth attitude is not necessarily a problem, but may indicate that the speaker is not taking advantage of the aditional opportunities that exist in the marketing sphere.

What are the opportunities? All this research is done with specific objectives in mind. Knowing your existing and potential markets gives you the chance to take action.

For example, once you have opened your mind to the point that most established businesses do not really know their markets (and new ones should not guess them), you have automatically stolen a march on your competitors. You have options which they have ignored, specifically:

- the chance to adjust the product to the market;
- information which might permit you to choose your customers for quality rather than quantity;
- the possibility of identifying new markets with similar characteristics, as yet untapped by your competitors;
- ways of expanding your existing market so that the whole of the new customer base comes to you.

The latter two points are extremely important because they suggest ways of avoiding the competition. Any action you take in the market-place which increases your penetration at the expense of the competition, even if your competitors do not know where the business is going, registers with them in the form of reduced sales and they will tend to take competitive action, in the form of aggressive pricing or other marketing action, which in turn can reduce your hard-won extra penetration. Expanding without alerting the competition avoids this problem.

The competition

At this juncture, we ought to consider against whom or what you are competing, because this knowledge is essential to your understanding of the market. Conventional thinking dictates that the competition comes from others selling similar or identical services. They are not necessarily in the same line of business, but the service is broadly the same. For instance, accountants and solicitors are threatened by banks which provide advice and support on tax, trusts and executorship matters, traditionally the 'product' of the professions.

Alas, in service businesses, there are wider threats. In a business selling a tangible product, it is relatively unlikely that your customer is going to stop buying the product and start building it himself. Rolls-Royce Motors do not suffer from this nowadays. Similarly, most microcomputer manufacturers sleep easy on this front. (Software houses may have the occasional nightmare ...)

In a service business there is a dual threat. With high-value repetitive services, there is often the possibility that the customer will hire somebody as an employee, to do the job in-house. Equally, with services of any value, you may be competing against a machine which, alone or aided by a cheap employee, can perform much or all of your service (all employees look cheap to the customer who perceives how much of your overhead is included in your price).

It is vital that you recognise the customers' options on these two fronts when assessing your competition and pricing or presenting your service.

There are opportunities as well as problems. You can sell your service against somebody else's product (or employee). Consider the better mousetrap. That product actually provides a service. The required result is that mice are removed. The customer may well prefer some means of removal which avoids the need for personal contact with mice.

The same principle can apply to the employee versus external service equation. Any employer concerned about the expense of having a low-cost employee sitting in high-cost city-centre premises may be very interested in a service which takes the task off-site.

You may even fight back against the intervention of high-tech. Some services which are carried out in-house on micro-computers may turn out to be false economy. Other low-tech machines may also prove less attractive than delegation to experts. Any housewife who has bought or hired the sort of carpet-cleaning machine which covers the carpet in damp foam and makes discontented noises as part of the process of removing dirt from the carpet may feel very warmly towards a contractor who will achieve the same end result by different, or any, means provided she does not have to be involved again.

Returning to the point about peripheral competitors, you need to use this knowledge to review your service, its price and its presentation to the market so that you do not inadvertently lose out to the hidden competitors or, worse still, make a case for them accidentally, by omission or by comparisons which unconsciously sell their virtues in parallel with your own.

Knowing they exist is more than half the battle. The accountants who are losing business to in-house microcomputers, which are, however, imperfectly understood and have unfriendly software, may be able to make a compelling case for an external service which costs more, but not that much more, because it is being done more efficiently with better software or by someone more fluent with the same software as the one the customer was running in-house. Opportunities like this satisfy our criterion about expanding the market without alerting the competition – making the market rather than taking it.

Gaps in the market

Those of you who have already worked long and hard on analyses of your perceived markets can be forgiven for thinking that some of these suggestions do not apply to your situation. This is undoubtedly true, but if just one of them identifies a gap in your researches, and therefore in your strategy, you may be able to drive a coach and horses through the gap.

Even the most rigid market can be expanded. Let us take a hypothetical case of a narrow service. Assume that your family has over several generations been supplying a necessary service to Members of Parliament. This market is of finite size and unvarying from year to year. How can you increase your sales revenue? If we ignore the conventional routes (pricing action, more frequent use of the service, additional services) we have to come back to market size. Contrary to appearances, the market is mutable. Could you sell to Euro-MPs? Could you sell to film and television companies seeking authenticity in their fictional or documentary programmes about the House? Would Ministers in the Lords ever need it, or want it for nostalgic reasons? Would ex-MPs need it? Would parliamentary candidates want it early, on the assumption that they are destined to be MPs shortly? Would foreign embassies buy, for fear of missing something, or because they are curious? Would major authors and journalists make use of it as part of their research?

Only one of these groups may be relevant, but given that

45

the target market started at less than seven hundred names, a few dozen additions represent a significant expansion in the market and one which your direct competitors may miss. The principle remains the same whether you are selling to bishops, owners of ancient buildings, rich family trusts, charities, judges, barristers, vets or criminals. Do not ignore lawbreakers as a target market. Socially tolerable offences (like bad parking) may have characteristics which permit the entrepreneur with initiative to sell them something. Remember too the brief flurry of interest in radar warning devices? And real or accidental criminals need legal representation. Marketing is not necessarily out of place here, even with one eye on ethical constraints. A minority of barristers and solicitors get the majority of criminal work because they recognise the relevance of this group to their target market.

To summarise, before you can make final decisions about your product, its price, marketing and delivery, you need to be clear about the existing and potential markets which can be attacked. Thorough knowledge of the targets can permit easier selling, avoid competition, utilise surplus capacity, change the quality of your customer base, reduce unnecessary costs, heighten user satisfaction and improve gross margins and net profits.

If you do not know who your customers are, how can you reach them or influence them accurately? If you do know who they are – or will be – you have a route to their needs, wants, psychology, motivation, buying power and their view of you and your sector. In this matter ignorance is not bliss, it is crass.

8   Communications

The key point to remember is the wide variety of media available ...

Getting the message across

There is a tendency to assume that communication is all about the media. Before considering the choice of media available, however, it is important to think about the message: what form it is to take and how it can best be conveyed.

There are several barriers to effective communication which must be removed if the marketing effort is to be successful. These barriers are set out below.

(a) If the message does not reach people, it is useless.
(b) If it reaches them but they cannot read it, the same applies.
(c) If they can read it but do not understand it, it is not just useless, it may constitute negative marketing.
(d) If it is understood but does not invite action, why bother to broadcast it?
(e) If it invites action, but does not encourage or facilitate response, negative marketing rules again.
(f) Recipients may be intelligent, but lack enough knowledge to put your message into context. Even geniuses can be ignorant.
(g) People are generally reactive, not proactive: for every one who bothers to find you in the *Yellow Pages*, there will be several who will not bother unless you reach out to them.

(h) Many people who need your services do not have the authority to pay for them (both in the home and in business).

There are solutions. For example, under (a), taking advice from a competent advertising agency is better than spending vast sums of money in the wrong direction. The problem under (b) is not just about middle-aged and older managers (company directors, perhaps) who need glasses to read small print, but also includes those with the most prevalent forms of colour-blindness. Very few designers bother to think about the colour-blind when devising arty presentations with multi-coloured typography. If you do not think about the problems of either group they will pass on to some other text.

Under (c), if the message does not tell them clearly what you do, it may irritate and certainly will not sell. Even if you and all in your immediate circle know that a picture of a chess piece and the words 'Bishop's Move' refer to furniture removals, thousands will be confused, particularly people new to this country who are most likely to need the service.

Under (d) the most common culprit is 'house advertising' – advertising designed to promote the company, not a particular service or product. If the advertisement is meant to influence the long-term consumer and can do this successfully, why not do it now? After all, by the time you could be reaping long-term benefits they might have died, lost their money, gone to jail or emigrated. Potential shareholders and the City are also supposed to be influenced by house advertising, but nobody has ever explained why they are not equally positively influenced by some demonstration that the company produces worthwhile service/product advertising which shows how good it is at communicating with the customers. Such advertisements may enlighten them more about your corporate activities than some brilliant but non-specific house ad.

Our concern under (e) is with the sort of advertisement which fulfils all the rules about inviting consumers' interest but does not make it easy enough for them to approach you thereafter. It is sad, when only a minority of advertisements work well, to spoil one by unclear or incomplete reply instructions.

Item (f) covers several problems. The first is that even if you specify clearly what you do, some buyers may not know what your jargon means. The same applies if your company name does not tell them what you do. If the service sells to people who have just come to a new job, new company, new house, new town or even new country, the risk of ignorance is dramatically increased. It is not their responsibility to become instantly omniscient so that your defective marketing becomes intelligible. You have to bridge the gap.

The point under (g) hardly needs examples but it deserves repetition because otherwise competent people in your team are likely to have a blind spot on this front. They have to be reminded regularly that the responsibility lies with the vendor, not the buyer. Managers have a capacity for repeating suicidal behaviour over and over again, like lemmings.

An unrelated example may help. General, marketing and sales managers are frequently tempted to establish branch offices in coastal resorts for reasons which allegedly have nothing to do with the quality of life for themselves and their staff. You will never hear them acknowledge the fact that half the normal catchment area is underwater.

Item (h) applies both to business and consumer services. Just as in the domestic situation it is preferable to influence the person who controls the purse strings, so it is in the business equivalent. Services and products above certain price limits may require the authorisation of general management or other less sympathetic parts of the company. This applies whatever the services you are selling. The golden rule is to influence general or financial management. General managers have the highest authority limits. Financial managers monitor the budgets of other areas and their approval may help you sell to the company as a whole. And they tend to be less rigorous about expenditure for their own area, if it is within budgetary limits.

The worst tactic of all is to sell into the wrong department at too low a level so that the person to whom you are selling has no authority and has to make the case for using you to someone at a higher level – badly.

Choosing your medium

When you are constructing a marketing strategy the message is paramount, but the medium is also very important. Its relevance and quality dictate both the receptiveness of the audience and the extent to which they bother to be an audience at all.

Some potential audiences are very unreceptive to the written word in bulk. A useful reminder is the Duke of Gloucester's famous reaction: 'Another damned, thick, square book. Always scribble, scribble, scribble! Eh, Mr Gibbon?'

The key point to remember is the wide variety of media available, for both the written and the spoken word. You can accompany both with pictures and graphs. You can use a combination of them or reinforce one with the other. Actually recognising that they are different is a big step. It is then possible to judge which is the most appropriate one to use. Most people, being reactive, just use the one that seems easiest in relation to the customer contact (or the marketing plan).

In practice, choosing the wrong medium may erode the impact of your message or even create resistance to it. For example, if customers expect a written response to an enquiry, they may be taken aback by a telephoned sales pitch. For certain services, on the other hand, they may be pleased and relieved because the phone call implies you recognise the urgency and importance of their need.

The spoken word can also be recorded, for playback down a telephone line or on a television screen. This is sometimes preferable to a dialogue between two people. It seems less threatening, and some people absorb a message better if they do not have to cope with the demands of an inter-personal relationship at the sale time. Perhaps this is why computer-aided learning works well. Try answering a phone when the caller is expecting to be answered by a machine. He or she is usually severely discomfited. So are people who have to compose a reply, at short notice, for an unexpected answering machine.

In the context of marketing, all this can be turned to advantage. The ideal is a sandwich, with the dialogue preceded and followed by the written word. The written word is the most usual way of making the first contact. It has authority. It can be retained. But it cannot talk back, reassure, react to body language or close a sale (unless you are selling off a coupon – relatively rare for services), and this is where a dialogue helps.

The third part of the sandwich is likely to be a tailored sell, formal quotation or confirmation of agreement. Its inherent authority and durability (people forget or misremember the spoken word) is now unique to the particular customer and reinforces more effectively the past process. Because it is to some extent de-personalised (no role playing) it may be more effective as a clincher. You can include more details than would seem natural in a dialogue. You can ask again for the customer to supply the reaction you require. In addition, the logic behind the price and product alternatives on offer can be more clearly understood by the customer in peace than with a sales person breathing down his or her neck.

There are further possible variations in use of the available media. The written word can appear on letters and their enclosures (direct mail), posters, television screens, cinema screens, magazines, newspapers, free gifts, balloons (hand-held, hot air or motorised dirigibles), streamers, carrier bags or even clothing.

Unless your service is so famous or fashionable that people will pay to mention it on their clothing or accessories, the more conventional media are recommended. The ideal medium clearly depends on the particlar service you are marketing, but some general guidelines may be useful.

(a) If your targets are readily identifiable, direct mail is likely to be more effective than most other media.

(b) If press advertising seems suitable, be very careful about your choice of publication. To take a fairly gross example, the sort of service which would be well received in *Private Eye* might be seen as out of context in the *Financial Times*, and vice versa.

Similarly, up-market services should not be marketed with cheap free gifts unless these are considered an acceptable gimmick. However, if you have a down-market service whose image you want to improve, a delicate upward progression in the nature and quality of your promotional media can help to reinforce the message.

For example, a betting shop which wanted to be perceived as a resort for gentlemen rather than for mug punters could improve the size and quality of its free ball point pens so that they looked more sophisticated and lasted longer.

Equally, a hairdressing salon which wanted to convey an impression of continuity and respectability might send designer Christmas cards rather than cheap pasteboard squares. My local one did exactly that, but forgot to include its address or telephone number – the message matters too!

Other variants in media include the quality, colour and texture of the paper you use in a mailshot. For example, reproducing your text on pink newsprint conveys an impression that it might be of *Financial Times* quality. However, copying the *FT* typeface as well should be avoided, as this could lead to legal action. Coloured stock, discreetly used, also helps people to notice (and remember) your message.

In summary, do give thought to the wide choice of media available. Do take advice. Do mix the written and spoken word. But do not confuse people with media which are out of tune with your service – accountants could give away free calculators, but not guides to gambling theory.

Public relations

PR, as it is often described, is much misunderstood. All too often the assumption is that PR implies press relations or at best media relations. Good PR includes media relations, but there is a larger audience and wider means of communication. That larger audience includes employees, shareholders, suppliers, customers, the media, government(s), the City and the rest of the public.

Communicating information to them about your organisation and its activities is a highly complex task and it is no accident that most major PR companies have established specialist departments, or even companies, to deal with the different audiences (or 'publics' as the practitioners say). The people who will advise you on how to present yourself to the City are not the ones who will deal with your product PR. At the beginning of this chapter you were advised to use an advertising agency. The advice about PR consultancies is not so firm, nor so broad. They have their uses and if your organisation is big you may find them, or an in-house department, essential. However, there are three problems.

(a) They cost a lot of money and, although they know more about PR than you do, they usually know less about your business.
(b) If you rely on the in-house department, it tends to hire external consultants to cover its own weak areas. This is expensive and again involves people who do not know quite enough about the business.
(c) What the public really likes is contact with a key operational manager or director.

These reasons for minimising the use of external consultants over-simplify the situation but the key point is valid: if someone senior in your operational organisation is willing and able, he or she may be the best normal channel for PR activities, with occasional support from outside. Shareholders, advisers, media people and the other publics generally prefer the organ grinder to the monkey. However, this approach, although personalised, must not be amateur or too informal. The various publics have quite specific and differing expectations of the way companies should present to them. The principle is that spokesmen or women need to modify the message they present and the role they play according to the subject matter they are trying to project, the medium used and the public at which their efforts are aimed. Being warm, approachable and possessed of human frailties may satisfy one group. Others may only be reassured by a mind like a steel trap, massive powers of oratory, a total grasp of the nuances of the business and ruthless impersonality.

However, the precise nature of the spokesman's role is secondary to the objectives and means planned. The key public includes anyone who is a potential customer or who may influence people to become customers. The aim is to make them remember your organisation, understand what you do and go away with a favourable image of your activities.

There are several possible views that such people may currently hold about your company and service:

● no view;
● a favourable, but misconceived view;
● an unfavourable view (rightly or wrongly).

Ignorance has certain advantages. At least you start with a clean sheet, unstained by misinformation, assumptions, gossip or past brushes with your van drivers. But all three attitudes need to be converted into an accurate awareness of your merits.

Total ignorance implies that your past public profile has been weak, that your name is uninformative or your activities unmemorable. Most people in business can name at least one company offering each service they are likely to procure. So can most householders. If your name is not on those mental lists in your part of the country, some image-building is probably required. The name is important. Unless, by other means, the company name has become synonymous with the service sector you trade in, there is a very good case for having a name that tells people what you do: Mac's Plumbing, Cope's Cuisine, Bun's Bakers, Eddie's Electrics, Wainwrights the Butchers, and so on.

Promoting the company name

How do you get the name across? Editorial comment is important (*see* page 65) and advertising may be necessary. Sponsorship helps and the *Yellow Pages* are effective once you have a good name. Visibility is also an advantage. If your service is performed on the customer's premises, find ways to expose the name. In an up-market service, your staff may not want the company name on their personal cars, but it must go on vans, uniforms and pieces of kit. Even the car problem can be solved by using magnetic name plates. Consider putting the name on the van roof. Most car parks and streets can be seen from above. Yours could be the first message visible from that angle.

The name is a very basic message. A more explicit formula is useful, whether for cocktail parties, local radio or the press.

As PR representative, be a figurehead for your sector. Preach best practice. State the obvious about your service and its benefits, but find some new way to say it. Consider developing a catchphrase. Several distinguished search consultants, not satisfied with being 'headhunters', say they are in the white slave trade. Insurance brokers, fed up with their tired image, may claim to be in risk management, with some truth. Find an evocative, brief and unique message that you feel comfortable with and, once you have arrested attention, you can add information and a soft sell. Most people can tolerate a little sales pressure if they do not think they are going to be bored, or lectured, or both.

A steady effort in this direction will enlighten the ignorant, reinforce the perceptions of the faithful and even erode the prejudices of those with unfavourable views.

Incidentally, if your company is a PLC or part of one, do not ignore the power of the annual report as a source of PR for the service itself. Many people read annual reports more avidly than the daily papers. Shareholders will often buy from 'their' company, provided they realise you are part of it and can understand what you do. A booklet called *Your Annual Report as an Aid to Profit*, published by The Institute of Chartered Accountants in England and Wales, indicates how much you can achieve in this area.

Public relations are compulsory. Your only choice concerns the nature of those relations and the influence you have upon them. There are good relations, bad relations and a middle ground of ambivalent relations. From the marketing viewpoint, ignorance equals bad relations.

All your organisation's contacts with and by its staff are components in these relations, and can help to turn ignorance into good relations and even bad relations into good. The internal PR department and the external PR company are, by comparison, a relatively small part of your total PR team, which includes every employee and even their families. Some attempt to influence their contact with the public is essential. For instance, tell them that they are the PR team. Tell them what face the company seeks to present to the public. Ask them how this can be achieved. Give them practical aids. In particular, remind them that every telephone call and contact with the world outside is a significant part of the PR programme. One excellent contact with you will be remembered against the background of your competitors' mediocrity. However, one insensitive contact can upset the good work of dozens, and unfortunately the bad impressions linger longer. Shakespeare, in another context, summed it up well:

> 'The evil that men do lives after them,
> The good is oft interred with their bones.'

From unawareness to action

The classic progression through which the potential customer is taken, from unawareness through awareness and comprehension to conviction and action is well understood – although some optimists feel that action should be virtually simultaneous with awareness and are usually disappointed.

Less well recognised is the potential for regression. Customers are human and there is a substantial risk of backsliding after awareness has been achieved. If you do not reinforce your position in the customer's mind, several things can happen.

(a) They forget you altogether.
(b) They confuse you with a competitor.
(c) They forget what business you are in (firms of accountants sound very much like firms of solicitors).
(d) They remember you, but you take second place to a newer, louder, flashier competitor.
(e) They remember you but wonder if you are still trading.

If your target market is small and accessible by direct mail, some annual reminder of your existence helps. However, this needs to be consistent, or negative marketing creeps in. A distinguished international group sends out extremely nice desk diaries but they arrive only twice in every three years. When they do arrive, they are very welcome and do not fall apart by mid-August (another negative marketing trick).

Handing out defective gifts is a serious fault. I remember *Time-Life* now not for their excellent magazines but for the free digital calculator watch they gave me when I last bought a subscription to *Time*. The average life of the strap was under a fortnight on the original *and* the replacements – enough to make you buy *Newsweek*. Images like this stick in the consumer's mind longer than reliable products and services.

There is a saying in my sector: 'You're only as good as your last assignment.' This is true of most service-based businesses. Worse, you may be only as good as your last ad, diary, newsletter, debt collection letter or warranty claim. One bad-taste article can make long-term magazine subscribers terminate their interest for ever. Rude credit control about a minor item does the same.

It follows that the process of creating awareness also involves maintaining it consistently, if you are to protect the chance of proceeding to action with enough of the target market.

9   Tools and techniques

The aim is to make the sale flow automatically from the personal relationship which builds up . . .

Selling

This book is dedicated in part to the proposition that marketing should make selling easier or unnecessary. However, this does not relieve you of the responsibility of ensuring that a sale does take place.

While the book is not a treatise on selling, we must cover certain neglected points. The first comes in the 'good news, bad news' category. In most service businesses the people who actually provide the service also have to sell it to some extent. Instead of the sale being handled and closed by a sales professional, it may be handled by an accountant, cobbler, engineer, lawyer, manicurist or plumber. This may be more of an opportunity than a problem.

It is probably easier to train the operational staff to sell the service they provide than it would be to train reps to provide the services they are selling. This is a gross over-simplification and unfair to many above-average sales staff, but the basic point remains valid. You must recognise the sales content of the operator's job and prepare your staff for it.

Fortunately, the person who provides the service understands it, is proud of it (if not you have a different problem, to do with recruitment or motivation), and should be capable of being trained to:

(a) recognise the need to close the sale;
(b) understand the 'two ways to buy' or win/win concept outlined in Chapter 4;
(c) negotiate, if the service is variable enough to permit this;
(d) bring his or her sales performance up to average levels.

This last requirement may sound conservative, and it is, but it should be attainable. Given a regular distribution of sales performance figures, bringing the below-average people up to what was the average line eliminates 25% of the performance gap between best and worst current actuals. None of these requirements demands that the service teams turn themselves into replicas of the old-style sales rep. However, they will have to discipline themselves to steer the customer towards a decision and, unless they are already being offered cash or being asked to whom the cheque should be made payable, will have to ask for an order. For those not temperamentally suited to the brash demand, the best way is probably to talk through the post-decision process so that the sale is taken for granted unless the customer fights back. Some examples follow.

- 'If you'd like us to go ahead, what will happen is that my disinfestation specialist can join me later this morning and we can have the place clear within the day.'
- 'You could expect savings in excess of £10,000 in this tax year. If you can give us authority to go ahead this week, we can guarantee to finalise the paperwork by 31 March for your signature before 4 April.'
- 'If Fred starts tomorrow, we can have it done before the holidays and clear everything away before you go.'

The seductive question

There is a reassuring technique for those service operators who do not quite trust their sales skills, even after training. This is particularly so for those who know their craft but suspect they are not extrovert enough to sell it. The principle is valid for all services but particularly helpful where you are offering something more than a packaged no-option deal.

It consists of minimising the number of statements you make and maximising the number of questions you ask. This has several advantages.

- It reduces the chances that you say things people do not understand, or understand but do not accept.
- It gets them talking, rather than listening to you.
- It makes you look as if you understand their problem and have the solution.
- It implies that you are not just interested in selling your service.
- By the time you and the customer feel comfortable that you have jointly analysed the need, the matter of closing the sale is often just a formality.

And that is the aim, to make the sale flow automatically from the personal relationship which builds up, using this technique or any other.

Negotiation

In my own company, the consultant partners were assumed to have the maturity and negotiating skills to set their own prices, rather than being rigidly tied to the fee structures in our brochures. Unfortunately, the consultant partners, euphoric at the prospect of closing a sale, tended to make concessions which weakened or even eliminated our chances of getting paid a fair price for our consultant time.

The following suggestions may help your consultants to avoid this problem.

(a) They should ask customers who want 'back-end loading' (i.e. no success, no fee) in the price structure to accept a *higher* percentage fee than normal in return for this concession.

(b) They should profess not to have absolute discretion in these matters. A tactical consultation with home base has three advantages:

- it demonstrates to the customers that the negotiation is being stretched to the utmost – good for their self-esteem;

- it permits consultation about a more inventive fee structure – or trade-off; and
- it gives the consultant time to think whether the deal is really worth doing at the requested price.

The technique of referring back to a higher authority, real or imagined, can also help to bring old prices up to the current level. It is more important to raise below-average prices to the norm than to raise above-average prices by the same amount. The relative gains in margin are greater for the former. Juan Manuel Fangio said that the secret of success in motor racing was not going 10 mph faster on the faster bits of the course but going 10 mph faster on the slower bits. The same applies to prices.

In the case of long-standing customers who benefit from special deals, there is a great temptation to leave prices untouched for fear of alienating the customer. This is wrong, for several reasons.

(a) They may already feel guilty about the price if it is obviously too low and be somewhat relieved when you raise the subject.
(b) Even if they are wholly resistant to the idea of a price rise for the existing service, the fact that you push for one should make them happier about the existing price.
(c) If you do not ask, you do not get. You need the price rise and asking for it is the only way to get it.
(d) You may be able to sugar the pill by offering a different variation of the service, with better gross margins.

The point in (d) is about changing the mix. In my business we actually sell consultant time and results, but the convention is to charge different rates for 'headhunt', file search, and selection from advertising. A firmer fee can be explained to the customer in terms of the mixture of headhunt (necessarily costly) and file search (less costly). This can still appear a bargain or 'most-favoured-nation' gesture while achieving the desired financial result.

A word on 'success only' pricing, still prevalent in employment agencies, estate agencies and the like. To some extent the custom of the trade prevails, but even in these sectors it is worth trying to get some front money into your fees. Any reasonable customer will recognise that you cannot afford to provide a decent service if your chances of getting paid are a lottery. A smaller but reliable sum on each contract is usually preferable to the random attainment of occasional larger sums. Never be bound by history. Always strive for the cash- and profit-generating route.

The way you achieve all this must depend on your relations with your customers. One possibility is to assure them, 'You always get most-favoured-nation prices. Nowadays, that implies £x.' If they do not accept £x, you can then negotiate by saying that you have authority to reduce the price a little to an amount nearer the old level by giving them a significant cash settlement discount.

Alternatively, for those services where part of the total cost clearly relates to recoverable costs paid out by you on the customer's behalf, while the rest is your net share, make sure that all the recoverables are fully declared rather than buried in your slice of the total price. Solicitors learned this long ago, and anyone can take advantage of the lesson. The technique has three benefits:

- it shows how slim your fees are;
- it stresses the inevitability of some of the costs; and thus
- it may permit higher *total* charges.

An A to Z of ideas

Advertising

Advertising is a very important art of marketing for many organisations but is sometimes misunderstood. It is not always essential and for many services may not be the primary route to new customers.

Lay understanding is further confused because there are two different types of advertising which form part of a normal marketing programme. House advertising is intended to promote the company rather than the service or product. Product advertising deals more specifically wih the company's 'product', which may be a service.

Advertising agencies love writing brilliant house ads. Unfortunately, because clients love reading them, rather too many of them get published. 'Too many' because they usually fail to demonstrate a relationship between the company and the product, and so do not necessarily fulfil the company's objectives. If in doubt, focus on the service itself.

I believe in advertising. A cynical observer might suggest that this is because I am in a business where the customers pay for the ads which, indirectly, attract new customers. That happy circumstance does not alter the underlying message that the advertising works.

Branding

Branding is the creation of a distinctive identity for a product or group of products. It is important for tangible products, less easy to achieve but perhaps even more important for services. You may think it unreal to find brand names, or perhaps numbers, for variants of the same service but it is virtually essential if the consumer is to perceive that the premium service does offer something extra.

It helps if the names are descriptive, but even calling one the 'old reliable' or 'original' recipe and the latest 'new improved' *Glop* or 'premium' *Sweep* must be better than nothing. This is not to say that branding is just about naming, but you need a name to hang the image on. Star ratings are possible: 'Five Star Gas Service' sounds better than 'Three Star' and is so intended. The 'Gold Treatment' is likely to be better than the 'Silver' and so on.

Even accountants, who used to split their product between audit and consultancy, now offer audit, corporate finance, human resources, management services and systems functions.

Motor dealers too have discovered that people who are too mean to pay for a full service at the right time will buy a short or intermediate service on the assumption that this will save money. Having apparently different products keeps the workshops fuller. And the customer has a clearer idea of what the product is.

Cold calling or cold canvassing

The Cold Sell is not recommended. *See* Tepid selling, page 78 for alternative.

Copy

Copy, the text which forms the content of your ads and direct mailshots, is crucial. If you have nothing worthwhile to say, why say it? It may just increase the potential customers' ignorance of your merits or their contempt for your marketing. This is one of the most important lessons in marketing. Good copy flows from a clear understanding of your service and your markets. If you really understand both and cannot think of anything worthwhile to say to the latter about the former, perhaps the service does not deserve to be marketed in the way you plan. On the other hand, if you are convinced of the USP and the market need, they deserve good copy.

Talk to customers, past and present. Ask people who use the competition. It only takes one concept, translated into good copy, to transform a campaign. Remember, or read, Townsend's *Up The Organisation* to find out, how much agonising went on before Avis finally decided that the only thing they had to offer in the struggle against Hertz was 'We try harder'. Remember too that mediocre copy may not just be mediocre in its effect. It may be counter-productive.

Corporate deafness

Being deaf to the customers' comments is not of course a technique, in our context, but it may be a part of the tactical armoury of people in your front line. If so, it constitutes a problem.

Your employees may play deaf unless you actively encourage them to listen and take action. They probably remember the messengers who, when they brought bad news, were promptly slaughtered.

The action includes:

(a) finding out more without seeming too negative; and
(b) responding constructively.

You may have to teach them how to do both. Without training, their worst human reactions may take over and they will either retreat from the customers and remain in sullen silence or, worse, imply that the problem is endemic. You should be able to remember a dry cleaner, estate agent, laundry employee or service engineer who has done this to you recently.

Editorial

Editorial mentions have certain advantages over advertising.

- They look more impartial.
- More people may read them, in the same medium.
- If they include enough data they may pull as well as or better than advertising in the same medium.
- They should be free.

It follows that they are likely to be cost-effective, if you can achieve them without too much effort or expense. It is generally not necessary to feed or bribe the press to earn a basic standard of editorial mention. Most specialist media and even some nationals are bored by the poor quality of press releases reaching them. If you can rise above the general level of mediocrity you stand a very good chance of getting some or all of your releases or verbal briefings into print. Your press releases should meet the following criteria:

- brevity;
- news value;
- relevance to the medium's editorial policy;
- novelty, if possible;
- exclusivity, if the journal is important;
- crisp, clear, simple English.

Fog index

You will find the words 'fog index' used in marketing as a measure of the intelligibility of marketing texts.

Marketing services

There is an official formula and a way of interpreting it, as follows:

(a) Take any 100 words of the sample text
(b) Note the number of full stops (x). Divide the result into 100 =

$$\frac{100}{x}$$

(c) Count the number of words *over* three syllables (c). Add to the result of 100/x =

$$c + \frac{100}{x}$$

(d) Multiply the result by 0.4
(e) If the final result (d) is 4 or below the text is intelligible to five year olds;

if d = 5–7, it is intelligible to six- to nine-year-olds;
if d = 8–10, it is intelligible to ten- to fifteen-year-olds;
if d = 11 +, it is intelligible to seventeen- to twenty-year-olds.

Given the variable quality of clients, customers and their families, it is strongly recommended that marketing messages achieve a fog index in the 4–7 range! Brevity, simplicity and clarity come as a relief, even to the highly intelligent.

Free

Consider the possibility that the primary response to your marketing could justify giving something away free, to retain interest. This could be anything from a blatant free gift, down to a free survey or equivalent, which carries the secondary message that the customer's next contact does not cost anything but time.

If you are in a learned profession you may recoil at the idea of give-aways but an initial consultation, without commitment, discreetly presented, can be very seductive to people who are overawed by your sector. A degree of discretion is required. Brash free offers may damage your image and constitute negative marketing, but nearly all services are in some way susceptible to this approach.

There is a snag. The wily consumer is now used to the fact that 'send no money now' offers tend to cost more than those where you have to put your money up front. They may assume that the same applies at higher levels in business services.

Gearing

Gearing is freely used in finance to describe the ratio between capital and borrowings. In marketing it comes closer to its mechanical origins. Getting a lot of mileage out of a fairly limited effort is what we have in mind and it can take many forms. You need to consider the potential gearing on all of your marketing efforts. For example:

- secondary readership of media;
- pass-on consumption of direct mailshots;
- recommendations from people who have been the primary targets of your marketing;
- the 'chain letter' effect if you were to write to all the friends of the organisation, like your advisers, staff, suppliers, labour force and so on to ask them, tactfully, to be part of your marketing effort (*see* Influencers, below).

Hard sell

The hard sell should not be necessary if your marketing has been done correctly. It can be counter-productive because buyers who notice and dislike the technique may develop and disseminate ill will. The soft sell is preferable.

Incidentally, the only people who really enjoy a hard sell are other sales people, who are watching the technique to pick up pointers. As the 'close' approaches they are more likely to offer constructive advice than an order!

Influencers

There are other words to describe people who recommend your services gratuitously but 'influencers' best covers the spectrum. They include:

- people who have used the service and recommend it to relevant third parties;
- those you have deliberately motivated to recommend you;
- third parties who have never used the service and may not need it but like something about your organisation or people. This last category includes everyone from your professional advisers to your doting relatives.

Influencers are very powerful, but not easy to harness, not least because those who have not used the service may not fully understand what it is. If they are known to you it is possible to correct this by direct contact or direct mail. If not, cross your fingers and hope.

Jargon

Jargon covers any words that people in your sector or company use and understand which are not fully understood by the outside world, in particular by your potential customers.

Jargon stops people reading your marketing messages or ensures that they are misunderstood. It is vital that you exclude it. Have all key messages read by an amateur who is not too close to the sector, so that he or she can identify the jargon and you can replace it with simple lay alternatives.

Even with the best intentions, words and initials can be understood by different groups of people to have totally different meanings. 'NSU' can be a distinguished German motor car to one person, Non-Specific Urethritis to another. 'Dr' means doctor to most people, debtor to accountants. Agencies can mean ad agencies to one group of people, but employment agencies to another contiguous group.

One piece of jargon which confuses even your employees is the creation of new names for customers for example, visitors, passengers, seat-miles and so on. Companies which talk about their customers by any other name tend to treat them less well than those who have this constant reminder.

KISS

KISS is an acronym for Keep It Simple, Stupid. These golden words are good advice in many areas of business and indeed, life in general, but never more so than when you are trying to achieve good results in marketing.

They apply to your communications with employees and with customers. They apply even more to your contacts with potential customers. They apply to concepts, plans, tactics and 'orders of the day'. That military phrase is included because it highlights one area in which the military have the edge over commerce. All the armed services have written reminders of things that have to be done today, whether routine or otherwise. Very simple. Understood by all. The perfect cure for the people who put off until tomorrow the very thing that somebody else knows is urgent today, but has not spread the word adequately. And the more important and complex such a task is, the greater the chance that it can go wrong, not just on timing.

In your business, the description of the service, terms of business, reply instructions, payment instructions, guarantees and advertisements can all be misunderstood, to create anything from non-communication to personal danger. All misundertandings are likely to involve the risk of commercial damage.

Lateral thinking

Lateral thinking is a concept popularised by Dr Edward de Bono. It offers a chance to improve your thought processes and remove yourself from the strait-jacket of traditional thinking, as taught by bad example in home, school and business life.

Its great merit is that it forces you to define the ultimate objective you seek to achieve and to consider whether there may be a simpler, cheaper, quicker or otherwise better way to get there than the traditional route. If you think for a moment about the objectives which people describe to you at work, or outside, even the most intelligent often specify a means rather than an end.

In politics, most factions which are against something really ought to go beyond this and specify what they favour, which will be achieved by stamping out their pet hate. This rarely happens: test the next party political broadcast you hear for this classic error.

In the home, it is very easy to forbid children to do something. Even if this seems a valid objective in itself, it is usually more effective to specify something constructive you would prefer them to do, or tell them the consequences of the forbidden act so that they can share your objective. (By consequences we mean the damage or nuisance you seek to avoid, not just the punishment you have in mind for them.)

At work, the easiest example must be the sales staff who specify increased sales as their primary objective, blithely ignoring the fact that the corporate objective is likely to be increased profit, which can flow from:

● increased sales volumes at the same price;
● increased revenue from the same volumes, by pricing action;
● static volumes and revenues, but better mix;
● better gross profits derived from lower costs;
● better net profits derived from lower overheads.

The wrongly specified objective not only prevents sales staff from contributing properly to the other routes to profit – and note they could influence four of the above five – but may permit them to distance the company from its objectives by gaining the spurious objective, increased sales, in one of the following unproductive ways:

● heavy overhead expenditure, which exceeds the extra gross profit earned: this heavy expenditure is usually on marketing;
● incurring higher direct costs or direct selling expenses;
● changing the sales mix in favour of lower margin items;

- starting a price war so that a greater total volume generates less gross and net profit overall.

Other problems can flow from blinkered (non-lateral) thinking. In recruitment, for example, some employers say, 'We want you to headhunt a new marketing director.' This is not a valid objective, although it may seem so to the people saying it.

What are they really trying to achieve? Presumably some improvements in the company's marketing? A new marketing director may or may not be the correct route to that objective. Even if it is, recruitment may not be the right answer. Even if recruitment is needed, specifying a headhunt is rather like saying, 'We want you to recommend the best way to get from London to Aberdeen – by rail', when there are patently other means of transport. Actually, if headhunting is wholly inappropriate, and it often is, the whole request is rather like saying 'We want you to recommend the best route from London to Shetland – by rail', but the futility of the request is less easy to see for an employer mesmerised by the headhunters' hype.

At this point the lateral thinker would also ask whether, as the true objective is profit rather than marketing excellence, more might be gained by saving the directorial salary and motivating the rest of the team better?

Other spurious objectives include 'best practice'. Necessity and best practice are often quoted as reasons for spending money or doing things dear to the sponsors' hearts. This is definitely an area where the head, preferably someone else's, needs to rule the heart. The lateral thinker will proceed beyond the bland words and try to identify the true objective so that alternative routes, or a more logical reason for the original recommendation, can be identified.

There are many applications for this approach in marketing, but they are most likely to be found in the progression from unawareness to action. Better ways of getting profits from sales from those who were previously unknown non-buyers are very welcome in most companies. In most businesses a totally open review of the options could include the following:

- doing nothing (except to improve the margins);
- making existing customers buy more often (or trade up);
- finding ways to identify potential customers more accurately;
- tempting them to volunteer themselves;
- changing the product;
- buying a company whose contacts are better than yours;
- making the sales and marketing people think differently about their roles.

The last option is not as glib as it may seem. If you could find job titles which remind key people why they are employed, without too much confusion, this might help. For example:

Sales Manager   = Manager, gross profit generation
Admin Manager   = Manager, cost-effective support staffs
Cost Accountant = Profit Engineer

At this point the purists may observe that we have strayed several times from lateral thinking *per se*. In defence of this deviation, please recall that lateral thinking is largely about straying.

Mix

The sales mix means the relative proportion of different services included in your total sales volume. It affects your profits because, as with products, the different services very seldom have identical profit margins, so if the mix changes within a static monetary turnover your gross and net profits will move up or down. If you are not aware of the movements in mix, the movement in profit will come as a surprise or, more likely, a shock. (Other things being equal, unforeseen variances tend to be unfavourable.)

It is one of the great sadnesses of accountants practising standard costing that it is virtually impossible to devise a variance analysis system which allocates a precise single cause to every part of every favourable or unfavourable change in profits. If the accountants are being honest about this, they might acknowledge a category of unexplained movements, which could be labelled 'mix variance'. If they are not, it may be desirable to find out where they have hidden the unexplained differences and how big they are. There will always be such a category unless the accountants are so bad they are fudging the figures randomly. You need to know, or your future marketing decisions are built on sand.

Negotiation

Negotiation means what it says. This is not jargon. The main reason for mentioning it is that there is not enough of it around. People in marketing and sales need to recognise that in a service industry the process of closing the sale can be quite subtle, and the marketing framework within which the sales people operate must facilitate some degree of negotiation. Buyers know your gross margins are wide and are quick to exploit this, if your frontline people are not properly briefed, or perhaps forearmed.

For instance, the hackneyed but effective choice between two ways of buying the service, rather than a yes/no choice, must be constructed if it does not exist naturally. Other grey areas need to be identified so that the customers feel they have negotiated too. Some possible examples follow.

- Buy now, pay later.
- Buy later, pay now (at a discount).
- Basic service or the premium one.
- If you don't want the widgets cleaned, we could do it sooner, or quicker.
- If you could bring it to us, rather than Fred coming out to you, we could save on the transport costs *and* do it sooner.
- If you do not mind doing the masking and preparation, we could finish it in a day *and* keep down to the minimum standard price.
- If your people could take it through to a balanced trial balance we could do the statutory accounts for last year's price.

You will observe that relatively few of the above involve a price concession. Passing on direct cost savings or holding an existing price level is possible, but other benefits are offered in most of the cases. Negotiation should not focus on price. Give them added value instead. Giving them something extra that would cost them £x at normal price, but costs you ½£x or less, is more cost effective.

There are other things you can play with, like:

- timing – sooner, later, quicker, slower;
- place – your place or ours;
- method(s) – within each type of service;
- people – perhaps they might prefer a particular employee for known skills or personality;
- quality and extent of service;
- type of service.

It is no coincidence that this list corresponds to Kipling's six honest serving men, What, Why, When, How, Where and Who. They can help you analyse other problems. They can also help you ask questions of the customers to determine areas where practical negotiation is possible with no damage to the profits. Doing things more slowly, for example. The vet who offers to operate on a patient and look after it during the post-operative period while the owners are away will save them the cost of kennels. The garage which *plans* to take its time with a service problem during your holiday and saves you the cost of off-street parking achieves a similar result.

Always find an area for negotiation. Lots exist, in trades as far removed from each other as accountancy and undertaking.

Off duty

People in service businesses are never off duty as far as their marketing is concerned. If you are awake you may bump into a likely customer at any time. Part of the art of marketing is to have a stock of throwaway lines which arouse interest and tell people what you do at first meeting.

Point-of-sale material

Most of us associate point-of-sale material with products rather than services, but there are many services where some form of POSM is desirable or virtually essential.

For instance, you will be aware of a motorist's night-mare called the Denver Boot or wheelclamp. You may not be aware, unless you have been clamped, that there are several flourishing service organisations which sell the victims a recovery service, saving them the time and trouble associated with the recovery procedure. Their point of sale is the clamped car. A persuasive marketing document under the windscreen wiper generates a very good conversion rate.

On a different plane altogether, many service businesses have more than one service offering, but are perceived by their customers as specialists in the one the customer first bought from them. Point-of-sale material can bridge this gap, with a target market which ought to be sympathetic to your blandishments. For example, most customers view dry cleaners as nothing more than cleaners. It requires effort at the point of sale to register the availability of repairs, dyeing and tailoring services.

Building societies suffer too. Many long-term depositors regard the societies only as a safe and comfortable place to put money. A significant minority would not think of going to them for a loan on mortgage. It is going to be an uphill struggle to educate all their customers about all the other services they are likely to offer in future – but point-of-sale material will be a vital ingredient in the marketing process. The same applies to banks, accountants, lawyers and brokers, although the 'sale' may be less clear cut than at the post office or building society counter.

Proactive

Being proactive is the opposite of merely reacting to events. As a technique, its application is much wider than most managers realise, because the majority of activity in most organisations is in some way reactive, as in domestic life.

People at work react to market changes, capacity problems, supply shortages, staff absences, labour turnover, cash crises, competitive action and so forth. Being proactive breaks this mould. Even in accountancy, that most traditional of professions, the proactive concept is recognised. It is called zero-

based budgeting. It means that you start the budget process with a clean sheet of paper, rather than being influenced by last year's budget, or actuals.

You could do worse than try some zero-based marketing. Sit down with that traditional clean sheet of paper and think how, if you were free of the constraints of what you are doing already in the marketing field, you would go about the business of marketing your service and whether it would be the same service. Having an intelligent outsider around who is ignorant of current practice might help.

Quality

Quality control ensures that your service meets certain pre-scribed standards. Quality enhancement means that you seek ways of doing things better.

The knack is to identify improvements which are suscep-tible to this approach and be sure they are needed in the market place. For example, 'better' may suggest:

- quicker;
- cheaper;
- cleaner;
- more consistent;

and lots of other things, all of which might be spurious in relation to your service. Your idea of 'better' must be what the customer wants. Take a photo-processing laboratory which moves from 48-hour or 24-hour turnaround times to 'in by ten, out by four' same-day service. It should increase its turn-over and can justify an upward price movement too. Going one step further, to a two-hour turnaround, may not be necessary for the majority of customers, and the minority who do want it may not be willing to pay for the extra costs and nuisance – or investment – involved. The same may be true of dry cleaning or any service primarily taken up by nine-to-five workers.

Similarly, reducing costs (doing it cheaper) may not affect sales unless converted into reduced prices, but it does affect profits favourably at once. One should be cautious about passing on the reduced costs unless the market is price sensitive and you can be sure of adequate extra volume. If you are cheapest already, or are thought to be cheapest, there is no point in lowering prices. You could even consider putting them up, because the lower direct costs will permit you to maintain or increase profits even on a slightly reduced volume!

Being cheaper is no good if customers want you to be more reliable, cleaner or quicker – quality, like beauty, may lie in the eye of the beholder so once again the need is to ask, and listen.

Research

Even if you have the most mundane product imaginable you need research, not necessarily into the service offered, although that can always stand a new look, but into your markets and their reaction to your marketing. It is essential that you explore the results of your efforts or the next attempt may be less effective than it could have been. This applies even if the vast majority of your marketing output is exceptionally good, because unless each and every part of the programme is equally good, you may be tempted to repeat the part you like the most. This immediately introduces a random bias wholly unrelated to results and may perpetuate mediocrity. There are so many variables in even the simplest marketing campaign that it is fatheaded at best (and suicidal at worst) to keep on churning out messages without making some attempt to ascertain which of the variables could be improved. The medium, the message, the product, the price and the time of year may all be capable of improvement. Anyone who has got it right already without testing is a genius, but if you do not test you are a fool too.

Solvency

Solvency is the state of being able to meet your financial obligations as they become due. People in sales need to be reminded about it. If you sell to people who do not pay, you become insolvent and the business may terminate. Everyone needs to remember that a sale is only finished when it has been paid for.

Tepid selling

There are relatively few services which actually benefit from cold selling, but marketing and sales people have an emotional need to rush from unawareness to a closed sale in one day. They need to be reminded that the very nature of a service business works against this. The doorstep sales rep knows that floor polish, brushes, soaps and toiletries will be bought for later use, but you cannot readily buy a service today for use at an unspecified future time. There is no shelf life.

Hence your marketing should achieve a situation in which the potential customer is aware of your corporate identity and service, well before the need for it approaches so that, with luck, enough of them will make contact with you, in person or by telephone, to ask more about the service or to buy, when the time comes. The old equation is that one volunteer is worth ten pressed men. This is still true, particularly with high value services for which the demand is spasmodic. Getting into the market's subconscious is a very useful preliminary. Much of the general marketing reviewed elsewhere in the book is dedicated to this end.

Uncertainty

All communication in marketing suffers from uncertainty to some extent. You can seldom be wholly sure about your service offering, the markets, your message or the media.

Equally, the customers may not be entirely certain about their motivation. This is why we laid such stress on research in Chapter 7. What you know they need may not be what they want. Worse, what they say they want may not be what they actually choose. In product tests customers will frequently fill in a form which indicates a clear preference for Product A and then happily take away Product C for immediate domestic use: this is why 'consumer clinics' offer them the chance to choose and take away one or more of the product samples, where possible. History does not record whether 'new improved' Coca-Cola was chosen this way.

However, you have to cope with the uncertainties at all levels. What is the solution? Knowing that uncertainty exists is half the battle. Do not be too sure that anything is sure. Allow for the likely range of uncertainty and you may steal a march on those of your competitors who are very certain – but partially wrong. For instance, experts and amateurs alike are fond of using the 'rifle versus shotgun' analogy when comparing the relative merits of different marketing techniques. The usual implication is that the precision of the rifle is to be preferred. However, students of the uncertainty school will note a fundamental flaw in that, although you may be able to identify with reasonable certainty that a particular person or group of people ought to be in your market, there can still be a lot of variables like timing, commitment to the competition and even price sensitivity which mean that you still need the shotgun to be sure of a sale. Perhaps a .410 rather than a 12 bore, but still a shotgun.

Visual aids

We keep coming back to the key problem with a service, that in general you cannot see the 'product'. For some services it may be possible to provide visual aids which show the service in progress or otherwise give comfort to the users. If your service is going to invade the customers' territory, a few 'before, during and after' pictures may reassure them that:

(a) there will be an improvement; and
(b) the place will not be ruined during the process.

If it is not that sort of service, how about a few graphs showing the potential improvements to be expected, expressed in money, petrol savings, staff turnover or ambient temperature? Audits and funerals still present a problem but even the latter are amenable to pictorial reinforcement.

Value added

This paragraph should not be shown to potential or existing customers because it exposes the big lie about added value. People think it implies that a product or service has gained in value by something you have done. This may not be true. 'Added value' merely means the difference in price between what you buy, in the widest sense, and what you sell. Edward Fletcher cottoned on to this over a hundred years ago. You may recall the lines from *Omar Khayyám*:

> 'I wonder often what the vintners buy
> One half so precious as the goods they sell.'

The price difference, then as now, is not value, it is what the market will bear. This concept is less easy to demonstrate in a service business but very obvious in a distributive one where the mark-up is justified largely by breaking bulk and distributing the goods to a point convenient to the customer.

The fact that you do not have to add value, just a perception of value, may come as some relief to those who feel unhappy about the price they are charging. If, on the other hand, it makes you feel guilty, perhaps you are in the wrong business.

X factor

Marketing people are always looking for the magic ingredient which will make all their efforts uniformly successful. Not quite the philosopher's stone, but along the same lines. Some call it the X factor because it represents the unknown, even for those who know they nearly had it in their grasp during the last campaign. Hence the tendency to look for, and worship when found, things like entrepreneurial flair, design flair (and indeed just plain flair), gut feel, and luck.

Almost without exception, these are illusory. Remember the distinguished golfer who, after winning a particularly hard-fought tournament with some exceptionally brilliant putting, was complimented on his success – and his luck. He accepted the compliment graciously but could not resist the temptation to point out the funny coincidence that the more he practised, the luckier he seemed to get. Lord Olivier was observed to be furious just after giving the finest performance of *Othello* that the spectators could remember from him or any other living actor. A friend asked why he was so annoyed. Didn't he know he had delivered the performance of a lifetime? Olivier agreed. He knew he had, but was livid because he did not know how.

So it is with marketing. There are specific ingredients which lead to success but, as Olivier well knew, it is impossible definitely to identify them and so repeat the success.

The people with an eye for design, any kind of flair, good judgement and luck have usually spent a lot of time perfecting their craft and/or have considerable intelligence, well directed.

Until the X factor comes along, it is best to settle for the W factor, which some call compliance marketing. It consists of doing all the conventional things well, in a disciplined fashion. It does not discourage innovation, if arrived at by logic, research, tests and validation. This involves asking What, Why, When, How, Where and Who, in order to do Well.

As hinted elsewhere, the people who rely on flair or an equivalent as their X factor, without analysing why they are temporarily successful, may find themselves wholly detached from their markets when the markets shift. At that point they may also discover that for some time past they had been detached from reality.

Zipf's law

G.K. Zipf's Law is more formally called the Principle of Least Effort, and is described in that excellent Penguin, *A Handbook Of Management*, edited by Thomas Kempner.

The principle states that 'Human behaviour is governed by an attempt to minimise the probable average rate of work required to achieve certain goals.' Sometimes this is done consciously, sometimes unconsciously, but most importantly it is not done often enough. There is another aspect of human behaviour to throw into the equation – the tendency of the apathetic to go on doing things the way they have always been done. Do recognise Zipf's Law, but remember you have to help it along a bit.

10   Meeting the costs

Make it a house rule always *to negotiate ...*

If, having read the previous chapters, you suspect that you could extend or improve your resent marketing effort, it is realistic to consider how you will pay for it.

There are several possible solutions:

(a) finding ways of doing it free;
(b) reducing expenditure in some other area to compensate for the costs involved;
(c) increasing the expense budget *and* the revenue budget because you are so confident that the higher spending will generate incremental revenue.

The first solution is considered further in The Free Alternative, *see* page 90. The third will not be discussed here since it could be difficult to implement in the middle of an accounting year and, in any case, the cynics will always fail to recognise the connection between expenditure and a favourable revenue movement. The results would be even worse if you failed to adjust the budgets: you could end up with an adverse expense variance for which you were clearly responsible, and a favourable revenue variance which was either swallowed up by someone else's shortfall or credited to someone else!

The second solution appears to be the most practical. It has the additional merit of reminding your staff that they can always save ten per cent somewhere. We shall come to some specific examples shortly, but first, two ways of proving the point that savings *can* be made.

Review a substantial sample of the bills that have to be paid by your company. Ask yourself the following questions.

- Why are we spending this money?
- How does it further our corporate objectives?
- Isn't it suspicious when an item is classified as a sundry or miscellaneous expense?
- If we cannot classify an expense, why is it being paid at all?

If you cannot answer these questions satisfactorily, you should ask the people who authorised the expense. You could also ask if there are cheaper alternatives.

Secondly, walk around your premises and look in the stock cupboards. Even in a service business, there will be the equivalent of a manufacturing company's 'non-production stores' – a network of desk drawers and cupboards probably containing stationery or computer sundries. It can be guaranteed that one of two things will be true of these stores. Either:

(a) there will be piles of obsolete material which should have been used up or sold (e.g. stationery with the company's *old* name/address/telex number/fax number/logo/colour); or

(b) you will find that you have been buying material that is too expensive for your needs.

Point (b) involves wasted expenditure. This can be accounted for by one or more of the following facts.

- Individual departments are ordering direct in small quantities and failing to benefit from volume discount. This means that nobody has bothered to research whether your volumes would permit you to negotiate a discount. Even if the volumes are low, there is always the chance of negotiating a discount in return for, for example, exclusivity, prompt payment or simply the fact that you have asked.
- Your staff are using the most convenient suppliers without researching which are the cheapest (and without re-checking, at least annually, that they are still the cheapest).

- Your staff are ordering branded (i.e. leading brand) items, rather than cheaper branded equivalents or 'own label' items which may be equally acceptable in use.
- They are specifying material which is too good for its intended use. Does the photocopier paper need to be 100 gsm? Wouldn't 80 or 90 be equally acceptable? Perhaps a better chosen weight would even increase the copier's reliability. Someone is probably ordering expensive quarto or foolscap rather than the modular A4/A5. Are your compliment slips designed to be cut from the A1 modular without wastage?

Do you always ask your suppliers how to achieve the same result cheaper? This carries the implied threat that you are prepared to go elsewhere if they cannot improve the deal, and they will almost invariably help, either by suggesting changes in product or by throwing in some price movement. If they do not react positively, perhaps you really should consider buying elsewhere.

This brings us to the crucial point. No matter who is doing the buying, make it a house rule *always* to negotiate. Never pay the asking price without a struggle – or a trade-off. An employee who is not happy with this rule should not be given buying authority.

Some more specific examples of how to avoid waste follow.

Annual report

If things are not too good financially, show your concern by having the annual report printed cheaply on plain white paper, with no expensive photographs.

Bad debts

Sharpen up your credit control to eliminate any debts about which you are at all doubtful: nearly every debtor will pay the most insistent creditor.

Cars

Reduce the number of people allowed company cars, the price limit on them, the frequency of replacement and any laxity in private use. You could even review the possibility of self-insurance for body damage.

Discounts stolen

Some companies, including sometimes the biggest and most reputable ones, take prompt payment discounts even when they pay late, or invent prompt payment discounts when your terms do not allow for them. Beware of this in your next price negotiation.

Documents

Many internal documents could do with a ten per cent cut. 'Masters' should be cut and pasted up if they stray over the end of a sheet, in order to reduce the number of photocopies. Binders and face-sheets are to be avoided, as are costly plastic spines when staples or 'treasury tags' would do. Do internal memos go in manuscript rather than typescript whenever possible? Do you photocopy relatively unimportant internal documents on the back of 'spoiled' earlier copies? Do you sell your waste paper? For more ideas, read the ICAEW booklet, *Decimate Your Overheads*.

Energy

Put the thermostats down a notch or two – the top five degrees may cost half your heating bill.

Flying

Minimise air travel, make sure the cheapest class is used, and that it is booked through the cheapest source. Do not let employees make their own arrangements.

Grand hotels

The same applies to hotels. Within the UK, consider the bulk deal with an appropriate hotel group.

Hard copy

Stop employees from making print-outs of data which is always readily available on screen, and make sure they do not photocopy it indiscriminately without a real need to do so.

Insurance

Perhaps you should aim for self-insurance in some areas (*see* Cars, above). Lean on your broker for more competitive quotations in other areas, indicating that his or her tenure may be at risk.

Journals

Cut back on non-essential subscriptions. Nowadays there is usually a free alternative!

Local sources

Buying from the nearest supplier may make sense if the distribution cost is high or you need after sales service. It may be worth conducting comparative buying studies wider afield and then persuading the local supplier to match the best overall price you have found.

Machines

Before you give in to requests for extra staff, consider whether a more intelligent use of the machines on the market could solve the problem. A 'memory' typewriter or word processor, for example, may answer the requirement more cheaply.

No

Some managers find it very difficult to use this word in response to requests to make minor purchases. Make it the norm, even if you have to make a standing joke of it: 'The answer is *no*, what do you want to buy?'

Nil

When budgeting, instead of starting from last year's actuals, work up from nil. Make sure each department really deserves its portion.

Postal costs

When mailing in volume, you *always* have a choice between sending it first class at the last minute and sending it second class a day earlier. Even sending it out at lunchtime rather than in the evening will gain a day, whichever class it goes. Especially at the weekend, when the mail is erratic, sending something second class at mid-day on a Friday is about as reliable as sending it first class on Friday evening or Saturday morning. Bulk mail should always be planned (and meet the plan) to be sent second class, or an even cheaper volume deal should be arranged.

Rail travel

Make sure there is a ban on first class travel and a ruthless review of payment of ordinary fares if 'savers' and cheap day returns are feasible. (Many employees regard it as a perk to charge full rates on their expense claims, having actually travelled at a cheap rate.) See if regular travellers could get British Rail discount cards.

Space

If you have been ruthless about the number of staff you employ, you should have some extra space. Could this be sub-let?

Telephones

Encourage your staff to:

- accept incoming calls so that they do not have to call back at your expense;
- if they cannot accept an incoming call, tell the caller to phone back (rather than offering a return call from your end);
- defer outgoing calls, particularly long distance ones, to cheap-rate hours;
- avoid private calls.

Unrecovered VAT

Make sure that all VAT spent, even on petty cash items, is properly documented and thus fully recovered (you might disqualify petty cash recoveries as far as *unrecoverable* VAT is concerned, if employees have failed to retain vouchers).

Cutting back

The purpose of marketing is to help the organisation achieve its profit objectives. Colleagues in operational roles do not always fully recognise the need for marketing, and regard all or part of it as a luxury. If the marketing department can demonstrate that better stewardship on the expense front is also a contributor to profit, the benefits will be twofold. The marketing staff will set an example of economy, and the effects will show up in their actual performance figures. If, in addition, they were to avoid spending all the money they had saved, the advantages would be even greater: in most companies 10–15% off the costs and expenses puts an extra 100% on the profits.

Looking at the other side of the coin, when the sales or profit performance is below budget, there is a tremendous temptation for people to spend even more money in an attempt to buy their way out of the problem. Typically, this happens when key sales or marketing staff adopt a 'sales approach', i.e. their priority is turnover growth. When such a situation arises, the symptoms include:

- more customer entertaining;
- higher travel costs;
- more price discounting (i.e. higher sales, lower margins);
- more money spent on discretionary items such as advertising and direct mail;
- more overtime.

Most of these symptoms indicate the employment of action as a substitute for thought. There are, of course, cases where you *can* spend your way out of downturn, but the fact that you are not doing well probably suggests that you have been spending your money on the wrong things. Spending more money in the same way as before is not a smart thing to do. A more logical course of action would include:

(a) curtailing all discretionary expenditure which did not have a proven short-term impact on profit;
(b) freezing or reducing the number of staff employed. Recruitment without general management approval and the employment of 'temps' should be banned;
(c) reducing 'non-production' stocks if possible;
(d) curtailing the power of junior employees to spend money – on travel, for example;
(e) re-establishing 'house rules' on travel, petty cash expenditure, private use of company facilities, entertaining,

purchase orders, authorisation of overtime, telephoning at peak hours, and so on. If there are no house rules or they are lax, issue clear reasonable new ones;

(f) finding ways of helping sales and operational staff to negotiate better, thereby increasing the conversion of enquiries into sales while maintaining or increasing prices, and thus profit margins;

(g) keeping all employees informed of what you are doing and why – most employees will concede that spending needs to be cut if they understand that the company is performing badly.

In the last example, neglecting to outline your objectives to staff may have damaging consequences. The constraints may not be observed because the employees do not know about them. Alternatively, they may follow the rules too slavishly because they fail to grasp the underlying motives. For example, cutting minor costs in an area which is crucial to sales performance will be wholly counterproductive. Sending invoices and statements second class will save you five pence on each, but you may lose pounds if the invoices are paid a week or a month late as a result.

There must be a balance. The negative effect of cutbacks can be considerable. Employees will be more willing to help with the economies if they see that constructive action is also being taken. If the management on its part is seen to be making considerable efforts towards the desired results, and the results themselves are clearly visible, the negative effects will be eliminated.

The following are some low-cost options which may be helpful at this stage:

● free trainees on the Manpower Services Commission Youth Training Scheme;

● cheap advice and research, by postgraduate business school students, for their projects;

● half price mailings, achieved by sharing the mailing with another company. This may have an additional advantage: it is easy to throw away one piece of paper unread, but several different ones require more attention.

The free alternative

However your business is performing, it should always be a matter of policy to establish the viability of a proposed marketing effort before agreeing to meet the extra costs involved. However, the ideal price for your marketing is free – even, to make a profit.

The best example of marketing for which you actually get paid is mentioned under Editorial (*see* page 65). If you can persuade a relevant specialist journal or national newspaper to commission an article, for which they pay, from you or one of your colleagues, there are several benefits.

(a) It costs you nothing.
(b) Editorial readership usually exceeds advertising readership.
(c) The article should increase the readers' understanding of your service.

There are some journals in which you might, at the end of your editorial item, offer a 'free' booklet about the services available in your sector. Through the money sent for postage and packing the offer could become self-liquidating or even make you a profit.

You may be able to recover the costs of a direct mailshot by sharing it with companies offering different services or products, relevant to your target market, and charging them for the service.